IMAGES
of America

GEYSER BASINS OF YELLOWSTONE

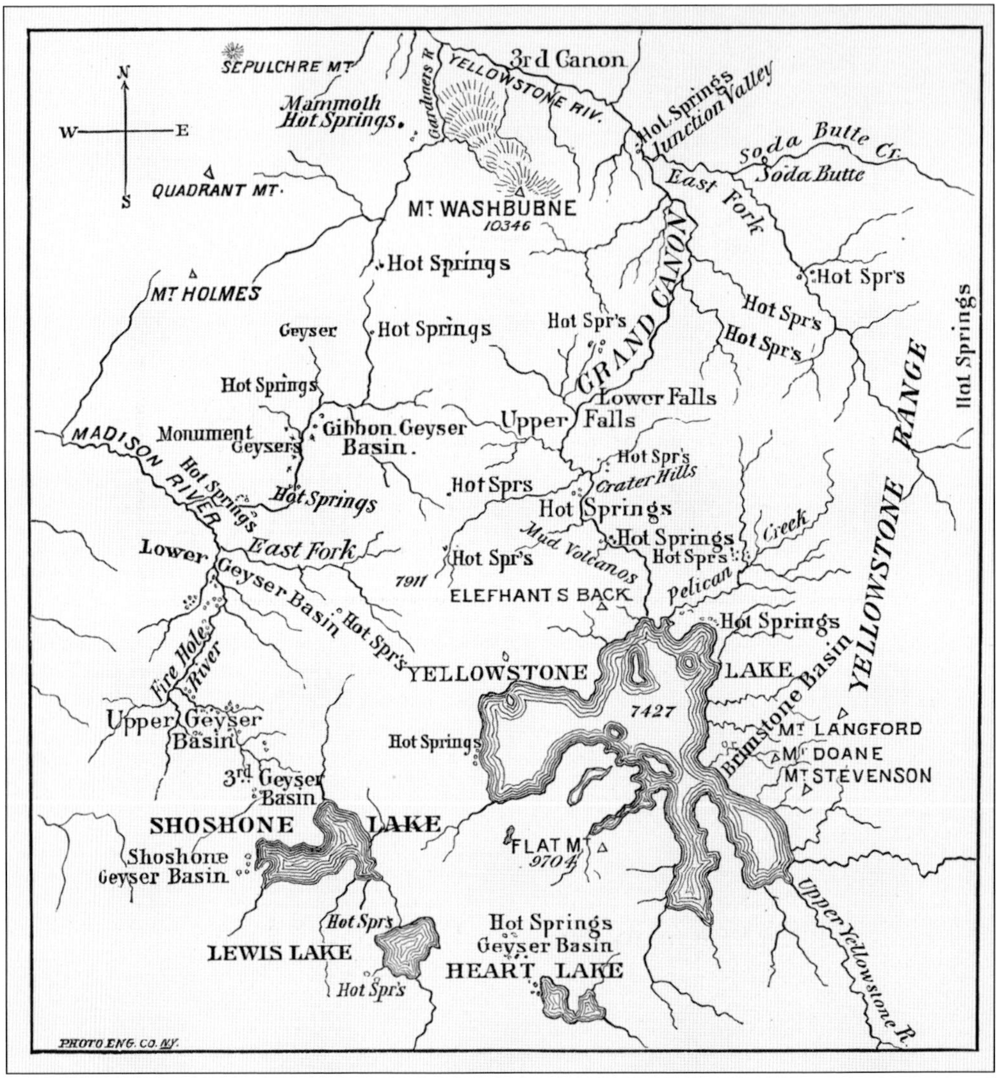

This map from the 1878 *US Geological and Geographical Survey of the Territories of Wyoming and Idaho (USGGS)* presents the distribution of geysers and hot springs in Yellowstone National Park. The 1871, 1872, and 1878 USGGSs investigated and published detailed reports of nearly all the springs and basins shown on this map. Since some of the geysers, hot springs, and basins are reachable only by long hiking trails and are without the safety of marked trails and boardwalks, this book presents only those basins reachable by the Grand Loop Road around the park. Since the earliest expeditions in 1869 and 1870 described the Mud Volcano area first, this book begins with that basin.

On the Cover: Around 1890, J.P. Iddings photographed an unidentified man posing in front of Giant Geyser in the Upper Geyser Basin with Bijou Geyser erupting to his right. (USGS, ijp00204.)

IMAGES
of America

GEYSER BASINS OF YELLOWSTONE

Dr. N. Genean Dunn and Thomas D. Dunn

ARCADIA PUBLISHING

ISBN 978-1-4671-3102-4

Published by Arcadia Publishing
Charleston, South Carolina

Printed in the United States of America

Library of Congress Control Number: Applied For

For all general information, please contact Arcadia Publishing:
Telephone 843-853-2070
Fax 843-853-0044
E-mail sales@arcadiapublishing.com
For customer service and orders:
Toll-Free 1-888-313-2665

Visit us on the Internet at www.arcadiapublishing.com

This book is dedicated to the early explorers and visitors to Yellowstone's geyser basins who provided vivid descriptions, drawings, and photographs. We also dedicate this book to the geyser gazer community that taught us about geysers and shared many amazing moments over the last 33 years.

Contents

Acknowledgments

Images of Yellowstone National Park appear courtesy of the National Park Service, Yellowstone National Park Museum Collection (YNPMC) and the Yellowstone National Park Digital Slide File (YNPDSF); the Carnegie Institute, publisher of *Hot Springs of the Yellowstone National Park* by E.T. Allen and Arthur L. Day (AandD); the Beinecke Rare Book and Manuscript Library at Yale University (BYALE); the U.S. Geological Survey Photographic Library (USGS); the Library of Congress Prints & Photographs Division (LOC); and the Yellowstone Gateway Museum. Images from the private collections of T. Scott Bryan, Udo Freund, Avon Leeking, Graham Meech, David Monteith, Pat Snyder, and Ralph Taylor are also included. All other images not credited above are in the authors' private collection. All images are dated, and the photographer is listed if known. Historical names no longer in use are placed in quotes. The authors thank Lee Whittlesey, Yellowstone National Park historian, and David Alberstein for suggesting improvements to this book.

INTRODUCTION

The earliest history of the geyser basins is written not in books, but in the rocks. The Yellowstone plateau was the site of some of largest volcanic eruptions in North America. Eruptions occurred about 2.1 million years ago, 1.3 million years ago, and 640,000 years ago. The last eruption ejected 1,000 cubic kilometers of material and formed the Yellowstone Caldera. The heat for these eruptions began in a hot spot in the earth's mantle and is the source of heat for the geyser basins today.

Well before the famous Washburn Expedition of 1870 left from Helena, Montana, Native Americans visited the Yellowstone plateau and probably lived in the area of the park as early as 11,000 years ago. Of course, there is no written record of these early inhabitants, but they left evidence of their presence, such as arrowhead-like points and chips of obsidian, at more than 1,900 sites. When white men first entered the Rocky Mountain area, they found that many Great Plains tribes traveled through this mountainous area. They saw evidence that the Kiowa, Crow, Blackfoot, Shoshone, Bannock, Nez Perce, and many other tribes visited geysers, conducted ceremonies, hunted, gathered plants and minerals, and engaged in trade in the area.

From the late 1700s through the early 1800s, a few hardy explorers ventured into the vast Yellowstone region. Lewis and Clark traveled within 150 miles of the park's northern boundary. However, they did not explore the rumors of volcanic phenomena up the tributaries of the Missouri River such as the "Yellow Stone." John Colter left the Lewis and Clark Expedition in 1806 and traveled throughout the region, but it is not clear if he saw the geyser basins of the park. A trapper named Osborne Russell left a written description of geyser and hot spring features from his trips in the late 1830s. After the fur trappers, the prospectors came in search of gold. One of these men was Walter W. DeLacy, who described some of the hot springs and geysers in the Yellowstone region.

However, not until 1869 did explorers set out for Yellowstone with the specific purpose of exploring its wonders. Charles W. Cook, David E. Folsom, and William Peterson entered the Yellowstone region during that year. They saw Tower Fall, Grand Canyon of the Yellowstone, Mud Volcano area, Lower Geyser Basin, and Midway Geyser Basin before leaving the area of the park. Word of their travels and the wonders they saw spread through Montana and led to the next and much larger expedition, known as the Washburn-Langford-Doane Expedition of 1870. This expedition named many important features of the park, including Mount Washburn, Old Faithful, Castle, Giant, and Beehive Geysers.

The next year, another group of explorers entered Yellowstone. This trip in 1871 was the first expedition led by Dr. Ferdinand Vandiveer Hayden, who was in charge of the United States Geological and Geographical Survey of the Territories. He and his party explored, mapped, and described the wonders they saw. Two members of the party, artist Thomas Moran and photographer William Henry Jackson, had to pay their own ways to be part of the expedition. Some of Jackson's historic photographs and Moran's paintings are included and described in this book. The idea of a national park evolved from these first expeditions. The US House of Representatives debated the "Act to Set Apart a Certain Tract of Land Near the Head-waters of the Yellowstone River as a Public Park" on December 18, 1871. After it passed the House, the US Senate approved the act on January 22, 1872, and Pres. Ulysses S. Grant signed it into law on March 1, 1872. In the pages that follow, information about the major Yellowstone geyser basins includes quotes from early explorers, employees, and visitors to the park. Photographs are presented that show some of the features explorers first saw, named, and made famous.

Following the government surveys in 1871, 1872, and 1878, visitors began to arrive. As the number of visitors interested in seeing the thermal features increased, the need for better transportation, roads, and hotels around the park became apparent. A road and hotel system evolved to support this visitor business. This book provides historical photographs that depict the thermal features in the major geyser basins, the series of hotels, and the means of travel through Yellowstone. In the early days, visitors were able to explore the basins with few restrictions. Walking around or over geysers was common. Standing near them and waiting for an eruption was an experience many wanted. As time went by, the need to better protect the thermal features, and the visitors, became clear.

Photographs in this book show many of the historic hotels around the geyser basins from the late 1870s to the present. The Old Faithful Inn and Lake Hotel stand today as a link to the old days of stagecoaches, dusty travel, and exploration. The location and changing sizes of these buildings indicate the changing needs to transport and accommodate the visitors who had traveled significant distances to see the geyser basins and other Yellowstone features. Stagecoaches served visitors to the park until 1917, and beginning on August 1, 1915, motorized travel was allowed in the park. In these early days, the railroads, and later the National Park Service (NPS), promoted the park to encourage visitor attendance. In the years following the advent of the automobile, NPS policy began to evolve. Promotion was less of a need. Improved roads away from geyser basins and means to define and limit visitor activity around thermal features were needed for the protection of both.

Some of the photographs in this book show the damage that occurred in the early days when visitors had complete access to the park features. Some old views show visitor behavior that is no longer permitted. Locations of some trails and roads are no longer where they were back in the early years. Many of the photographs taken then cannot be re-created today because the locations are not accessible for safety reasons and for protection of the rare features.

Yellowstone is a remarkable place that is visited by people from around the world. By 1992, approximately three million visitors traveled annually to "Wonderland," as Yellowstone has often been called. It is a wonder that these numbers can be accommodated, given that most folks come between June and September. This book celebrates Yellowstone's rich geyser history through historic photographs. The people who came to explore and survey the park, the people who protected the park, and the visitors who loved the park so much that they braved difficult travel and living conditions to see it are also to be celebrated as a part of Yellowstone's rich past. Let future historians who look back still have today's spectacular features to reflect upon. Please help protect these thermal features for the children and adults who have yet to be amazed by the sites and smells of Yellowstone's geyser basins.

One

Mud Volcano

The mountain men and fur trappers of the early 1800s told tales of strange phenomena like boiling water, spouting fountains, mud pools smelling of brimstone, and hot steam released from the ground. These tales piqued the interest of early explorers. In 1859, Capt. William F. Raynolds of the US Army was sent to explore the region of the principal tributaries of the Yellowstone River, including the Gallatin and Madison forks of the Missouri River. Based on his report, his expedition encircled the region of the Upper Yellowstone but did not penetrate it.

In 1869, David E. Folsom, C.W. Cook, and William Peterson journeyed into the Yellowstone region, shared their experiences with friends, and wrote of their adventures in the Chicago publication *Western Monthly* in July 1870. Based on this report, a larger expedition was launched, the Washburn Expedition of 1870. Nine Helena, Montana, residents commenced their expedition, obtained a military escort at Fort Ellis, and departed for the Yellowstone region on August 22, 1870. Upon their return on September 27, 1870, the explorers wrote many articles. Nathaniel P. Langford's account in *Scribner's Monthly* in May and June 1871 provided detailed descriptions as well as numerous woodcuts illustrating their adventures. As a result of the Washburn Expedition, the government launched joint expeditions in 1871—one led by Capt. John W. Barlow and Capt. David P. Heap to explore and map the region and one led by Ferdinand V. Hayden, who had accompanied Raynolds in 1859, to observe and document the features of the area. The writings of these explorers, especially those from the Washburn Expedition and the USGGS of 1871, led Congress to set aside the entire area as a national park on March 1, 1872.

Hayden led two more expeditions under the auspices of the USGGS in 1872 and 1878. The expeditions of 1871, 1872, and 1878 were documented by in-depth reports with maps, drawings, and descriptions of thermal, geographic, and geological features and with photographs by William Henry Jackson and artistic renderings of thermal features by Thomas Moran.

Although Jim Bridger (depicted in this woodcut), guide for Captain Raynolds, told tales regarded by some as lies, his accounts rang true. When Raynolds wrote of Bridger's "immense boiling spring," he pointed out, "As he is uneducated, and had probably never heard of the existence of such natural marvels elsewhere [such as Iceland], I have little doubt that he spoke of that which he had actually seen." (NPS Archives.)

David E. Folsom, C.W. Cook, and William Peterson, seen here from left to right, set out for a six-week trip on September 6, 1869. They journeyed from Fort Ellis, near present-day Bozeman, Montana, and generally followed the path of the Yellowstone River. On September 21, they arrived at the Upper and Lower Falls. (YNPDSF, 02954 [Folsom], 02953 [Cook], and 02956 [Peterson], respectively.)

Folsom writes that "the hills crowd in on either side forcing the water into a narrow channel, through which it hurries with increasing speed, until, rushing through a chute sixty feet wide, it falls in an unbroken sheet over a precipice 115 feet [109 feet] in height." The Upper Falls flow over volcanic rocks more resistant to erosion than the downstream rocks, which are hydrothermally altered. (Stanley, 1880.)

THE UPPER FALL, YELLOWSTONE.

Folsom continues his narrative, writing that the Yellowstone River "widens out again, flows with steady course for half a mile between steep timbered bluffs 400 feet high, and again narrowing in till it is not more than 75 feet wide, it makes the final fearful leap of 350 feet [308 feet]." The next day, the Folsom-Cook-Peterson Expedition resumed its journey, arriving at the Mud Volcano area. (Haynes, 1887.)

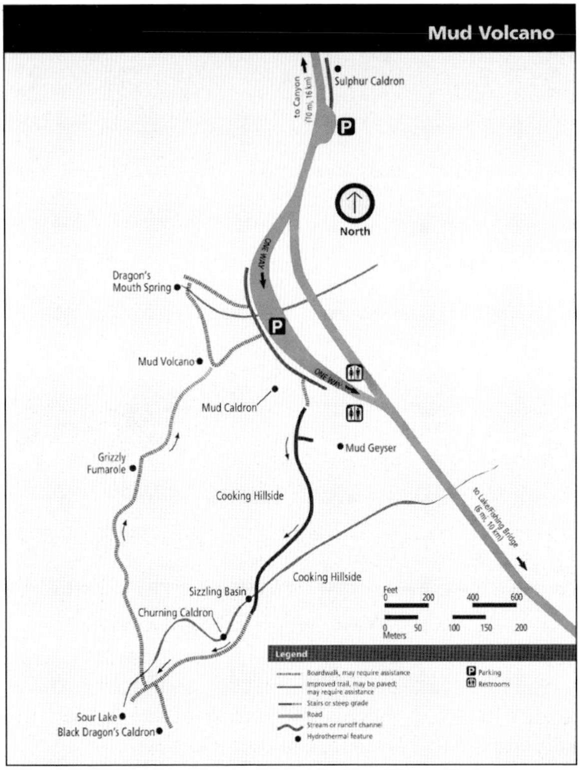

This map shows the location of features in Mud Volcano. Early explorers described the features of Mud Geyser (shown below), Mud Volcano, and Dragon's Mouth. Langford describes Mud Geyser: "It presents a funnel-shaped orifice, in the midst of a basin 150 feet in diameter . . . . The crater . . . is 30 x 50 feet in diameter. It tapers quite uniformly to the depth of about 30 feet . . . The flow of this geyser is regular every six hours. The water rises gradually, commencing to boil when about half way to the surface . . . When the crater is filled, it is expelled from it in a splashing, scattered mass, 10 or 15 feet in thickness, to a height of 40 feet." The geyser was known to be active from the early expeditions in 1869 through the turn of the century and may have erupted in 1922. (Left, NPS brochure; below, *Scribner's Monthly*, 1871.)

E.T. Allen and Arthur L. Day extensively studied many of the thermal features in Yellowstone from 1925 to 1932 and published their detailed reports in *Hot Springs of the Yellowstone National Park* in 1935. They state, "That it [Mud Geyser] actually erupted to 20 or 30 feet in the seventies [1870s] seems to be beyond question, but we have heard of no livelier activity than it shows now for many years. It seems highly probable that the impermanent character of this geyser was due to the nature of the ground in which it occurred; a steam reservoir in clay or gravel, not cemented by sinter, could hardly be expected to remain intact for any great length of time." (Above, *USGGS*, 1878; below, AandD.)

1305. Mud Geyser and Mud Volcano in Distance, Yellowstone Park.

Visitors walk around the edge of Mud Geyser and head up toward Mud Volcano in the view at left from before 1915. In the summer and fall of 1978, swarms of shallow small earthquakes occurred in the Mud Volcano area. Old features frothed, new features popped up, and trees began to die. In 1993, soil temperatures rose again, and more trees died in the area around the geyser's south end. In January 1995, more steam vents and shallow pools sizzled. In 1999, mud pots formed and then exploded, leaving a deep hole. The image below of Mud Geyser in 2005 shows the increased activity on the south side of the area. (Left, YNPMC, YELL #147785; below, photograph by the authors, 2005.)

Early traveler Rev. Edwin J. Stanley described Mud Volcano: "guided by an immense jet of steam, and attended with thunder-like reports, loud enough to be heard half a mile, we soon came to a horrible-looking pit in a grove on the slope of the hill . . . One shrinks back with fear as he peeps into the fearful cauldron . . . where at a depth of 40 feet, the dark, paint-like fluid boils and gurgles with a constant roar, which makes the earth tremble under his feet, sending up volumes of steam, which can be seen for miles, and emitting the same villainous fumes that characterize all of these horrible caldrons." Today, Mud Volcano is quieter, and the water levels have subsided, but the water and the heavy gas discharge continue to undercut the back wall. (Above, Weed, 1929; below, photograph by the authors, 2012.)

Reverend Stanley describes what he calls "Giant's Caldron": "Not far from here, just down the hill, there is a vast cavern, the size and entrance of which are covered with a soft, greenish sediment, deposited from mineral-charged gases . . . The roof, though at the mouth sufficiently elevated to admit a man of full stature, slopes gradually backward to the water's edge. Though we confess a good share of curiosity, we forbear to enter here, being met by huge bursting bubbles of water dashing against the roof of the cavern, emitting forcible volumes of sulfurous steam, soon driving us from the place." In early guidebooks from 1912 and 1916, this feature is called "Green Gable Spring," but within a decade it carried its present name, Dragon's Mouth Spring. Kiowa tribal stories say that a hot spring called Dragon's Mouth is where their creator gave them the Yellowstone area for their home. (Photograph by the authors, 2012.)

Two

Mammoth Hot Springs and Touring the Geyser Basins

The 1871 and 1872 government expeditions left from Fort Ellis near present-day Bozeman, Montana. Instead of following the Yellowstone River, they headed south near present-day Gardiner, Montana, following the Gardner River, a tributary of the Yellowstone. Choosing this new route, the 1871 expedition discovered Mammoth Hot Springs. Both expeditions then returned to the Yellowstone River, observing Tower Fall, climbing Mount Washburn, and stopping at the Upper and Lower Falls. They investigated Mud Volcano and traveled around the western edge of the Yellowstone Lake, visiting West Thumb Geyser Basin. Wanting to see the geyser basins of the Fire Hole River described by the earlier explorers, they traveled across Hayden Valley and the Central Plateau, arriving at and exploring the Lower, Midway, and Upper Geyser Basins. As a result, Norris Geyser Basin was not explored by either the 1871 or 1872 USGGS.

E.S. Topping, an early explorer and historian, claimed credit for discovering Norris Geyser Basin. In *Chronicles of the Yellowstone*, he reports that in July 1872, "a few days after Hayden had left the Mammoth Hot Springs on his way up the [Yellowstone] river, Dwight Woodruff and E.S. Topping . . . went up the Gardner River. The latter went up on Observation mountain [probably 8,257-foot-high Bunsen Peak] . . . At daylight next morning, he saw, far to the south, an immense column of steam arising through the still air. [They] . . . went through the intervening woods, and at noon of the second day found a geyser basin, heretofore unknown. This is now called the Norris Basin . . . . The two returned to the Mammoth Hot Springs and told of their discovery." As a result, the government survey of 1878 explored Norris Geyser Basin and other basins.

As travelers began to arrive in the newly created national park to see the wonders of the geysers, the need for transportation to the park, roads, vehicles to transport the travelers around the park, and food and lodging became evident. The early park superintendents began planning visitor travel to the geyser basins.

After the Washburn Expedition, Nathaniel P. Langford (pictured) promoted building an extension of the Northern Pacific Railroad (NPRR) to bring travelers to Yellowstone. According to Alfred Runte in *Trains of Discovery*, the NPRR funded some of the costs of the exploration of Yellowstone, most notably the costs for Thomas Moran to accompany the USGGS. The NPRR promoter and financier sent a letter to Dr. Hayden proposing the introduction of legislation to create the national park. In 1872, Langford was appointed the first superintendent of Yellowstone National Park. (YNPDSF, 09583.)

Road building commenced in 1878 under the direction of the second civilian superintendent of Yellowstone, Philetus W. Norris (pictured). He is credited with the general plan of the Grand Loop Road, which linked all the major geyser basins and points of interest. Hiram Chittenden of the Army Corps of Engineers took charge of road construction in 1891; by 1906, the Grand Loop Road was completed. (YNPDSF, 02958.)

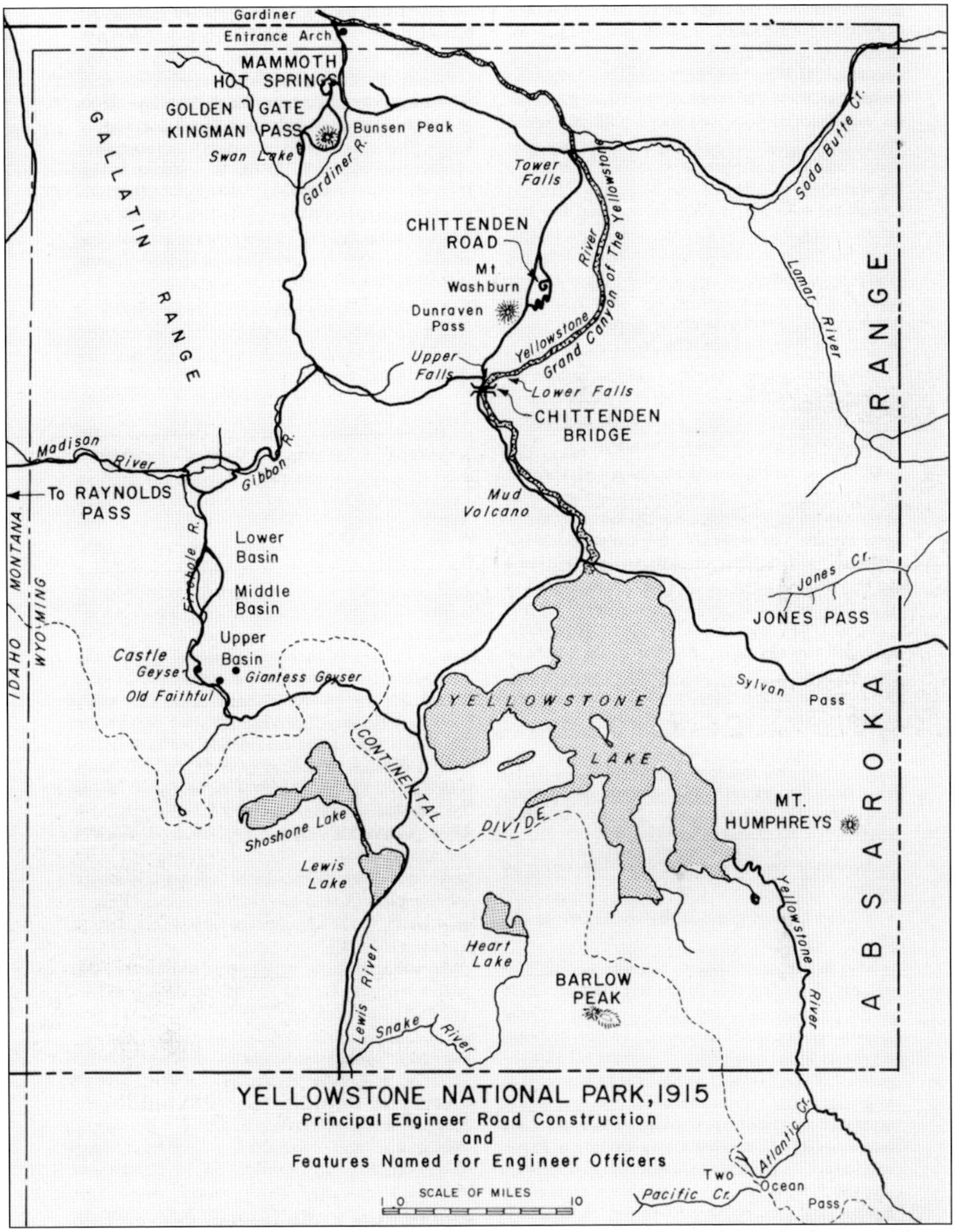

This map from 1915 shows the principal road construction around and through the geyser basins in Yellowstone National Park, known as the Grand Loop Road. The main geyser basins labeled on the map include Upper, Middle (now Midway), and Lower Basins. Not shown on the map, Norris Geyser Basin is located west of the junction of the Gibbon River and the road north to Mammoth Hot Springs. West Thumb Geyser Basin sits where the road from Old Faithful intersects the road along Yellowstone Lake. This basic road configuration closely represents the roads today. Among other construction, Hiram Chittenden built the stone entrance arch at the Northern Entrance, the concrete viaduct in Golden Gate Canyon, and the road through the Hoodoos; he built the steel and concrete arch bridge near Canyon and the road to the summit of Mount Washburn. (*Enchanted Enclosure*, Kenneth H. Baldwin, 1976.)

By 1883, the Northern Pacific Railroad completed a rail line to Cinnabar, Montana, and by 1903 a spur line ran to Gardiner, Montana, as shown above. Olin Wheeler, in *Sketches of Wonderland*, an illustrated advertising brochure for the NPRR published in 1895, lists the cost of a round-trip NPRR ticket from St. Paul, Minnesota, to Livingston, Montana, at $47.50. For another $47.50, a traveler could go from Cinnabar to Mammoth, to all the geyser basins, to Yellowstone Lake, to the Upper and Lower Falls, and return. This included all rail and stagecoach transportation with five-and-a-half-days accommodations at the hotels. Travelers entered the park through the entrance arch outside Gardiner, shown below, where Pres. Theodore Roosevelt placed the cornerstone in 1903. (Above, American News postcard no. 5483, 1907; below, Detroit postcard no. 7816, 1915.)

By 1886, the Yellowstone National Park Transportation Company had a fleet of sightseeing vehicles (above). The larger six-horse tallyho stagecoaches transported visitors from the train depot in Cinnabar, or, later, in Gardiner, Montana, to the hotels at Mammoth Hot Springs and other park locations. The stagecoaches entered through the Gardiner entrance station (shown above), and traveled along the Gardner River to Mammoth Hot Springs, passing by the Eagle Nest Rock (pinnacle seen in the center background at right), a notable feature in early travel photographs. Yellowstone observation wagons, which had four-horse teams, were then used to take visitors on the "Grand Loop" tour through the park. (Above, Bloom Brothers postcard no. R57438, 1915; right, Detroit postcard no. 8812, 1910.)

Seen above is the earliest accommodation at Mammoth Hot Springs, the McCartney Hotel, built in 1871. This was the first hotel in Yellowstone National Park. The structure burned in late 1912 after use as a laundry. By 1883, the National Hotel, seen below, was built. According to Capt. John Pitcher, acting superintendent in 1901, "Much time and money have been expended in improving the exterior appearance and modernizing the interior of this structure . . . painted a terra-cotta color with brown trimmings . . . a new covered loading platform . . . two new bathrooms on each floor . . . 200 electric lights, and a new and modern steam-heating plant, with radiators in every room." A third hotel, the Cottage Hotel, opened to visitors in 1885. (Above, YNPDSF, 10594, Robert Robinson; below, BYALE, 1065785, 1885, F. Jay Haynes.)

Once at Mammoth, the visitors explored the many features of Mammoth Hot Springs, including the hot springs terraces, depicted above. The image below shows Marble Terrace with Fort Yellowstone in the background. Reverend Stanley again offers a description: "This immense calcareous formation, with its numberless and intricate phenomena . . . is the chief object of interest here . . . On each level, or terrace, there is a large central spring, which is usually surrounded by a basin of several feet in diameter, and the water, after leaving the main basin at different portions of the delicately-wrought rim, flows down the declivity, step by step, forming hundreds of basins and reservoirs of every size and depth . . . their margins beautifully scalloped with a finish resembling bead-work of exquisite beauty." (Above, 1878 *USGGS;* below, Detroit chromolithograph no. 53323, 1902.)

As seen above, after visitors explored Mammoth Hot Springs, they climbed aboard the four-horse touring stagecoaches at the National Hotel in Mammoth to head toward Norris Geyser Basin. A *1923 Campbell Guide* describes the hotel as "superbly located on the plaza facing Fort Yellowstone, with scenic surroundings beyond compare." Over the years, the National Hotel received a renovation, as seen below in this 1923 postcard, and became known as the Mammoth Hotel. By the mid-1930s, this structure was razed and the Mammoth Hot Springs Hotel complex that stands today was built. In addition, Mammoth Lodge was built across from the terraces in 1917 by the Yellowstone Park Camping Co. (Above, Detroit postcard no. 8801, 1907; below, Bloom Brothers postcard no. YP63, 1917.)

As visitors headed to the geyser basins, stagecoaches traveled across a wooden trestle built in 1885, as seen above. After crossing the trestle, stagecoaches passed through Golden Gate Canyon by Rustic Falls, shown below. By 1900, Chittenden built the concrete Golden Gate Viaduct, making travel much safer and easier. The Golden Gate Viaduct was widened and strengthened in 1933. As the *1923 Campbell Guide* describes, "at its departure at the brink of Rustic Falls . . . [the traveler] rolls out into the open, over a level road leading straight away through the meadows . . . on the right is Swan Lake . . . all around . . . the foothills rise to snow-capped peaks." This included Electric Peak, the tallest peak of the Gallatin Range at 10,969 feet. (Above, YNPDSF, 02917; below, BYALE, 1065995, T.W. Ingersoll, 1885.)

William W. Wylie offered tours beginning in 1881. In 1896, he received a franchise to provide tours through the park and house the visitors in permanent tent camps; in 1898, a weeklong Wylie tour cost $35. Those traveling the "Wylie Way" stopped at the Swan Lake Camp south of Golden Gate Canyon, as seen above. Below is a Wylie's Swan Lake Camp compartment tent used from 1893 to 1916. In addition to this camp, by 1915 Wylie Way camps included Yellowstone Camp (near the West Entrance), Upper Geyser Basin Camp, Lake Camp (near the current Lake Lodge site), Cody Camp (near the East Entrance), Canyon Camp (near Artist Point), and Roosevelt Camp. Wylie also ran the Gibbon and Thumb Lunch Stations. Other camping companies evolved during the history of the park, and cabins eventually replaced tents. (Above, YNPDSF, 02817; below, Wylie postcard.)

Three

Norris Geyser Basin

Albert C. Peale completed the first in-depth description of the features at Norris Geyser Basin as part of the 1878 *USGGS*. Intrigued by the photographs, artwork, and stories of the early explorers, private parties began to visit and write about Yellowstone and its famous geyser basins between 1872 and 1878. These included Rev. Edwin J. Stanley, who wrote *Rambles in Wonderland*; Windham Thomas Wyndham-Quin, the Earl of Dunraven, who wrote *The Great Divide*; and Gen. William E. Strong, who wrote *A Trip to the Yellowstone National Park*. However, none of these visitors saw Norris Geyser Basin. As described in the first chapter, Allen and Day spent part of seven years, from 1925 to 1932, studying the hot springs of Yellowstone. Their studies included Norris Geyser Basin. More recently, Donald E. White, R.A. Hutchinson, and T.E.C. Keith studied and summarized most of the research on Norris Geyser Basin, publishing *The Geology and Remarkable Thermal Activity of Norris Geyser Basin, Yellowstone National Park, Wyoming*, USGS Professional Paper 1456, in 1988.

According to White, Hutchinson, and Keith, Norris Geyser Basin is the most interesting and diverse thermal area in the park for several reasons:

> 1. The basin includes most varieties of hot springs, geysers, fumaroles, and mud volcanoes found elsewhere in the park. Only travertine depositing springs, such as those at Mammoth Hot Springs are absent. Steamboat Geyser is the park's highest erupting geyser of historical record; Black Growler fumaroles have the highest recorded surface temperature; and research drill hole Y-12 has the highest temperature yet measured in the park and also has the highest temperature yet recorded for its depth in world geothermal systems (excluding volcanoes and directly related volcanic fumaroles). 2. Norris Basin displays a wide variety of chemical types of waters, precipitates, and altered rocks, including nearly the total range found elsewhere in the park. 3. The area demonstrates the longest history of thermal activity of any of the major geyser basins. 4. Changes in activity in Norris Basin occur more frequently and often more vigorously than in other Yellowstone thermal areas.

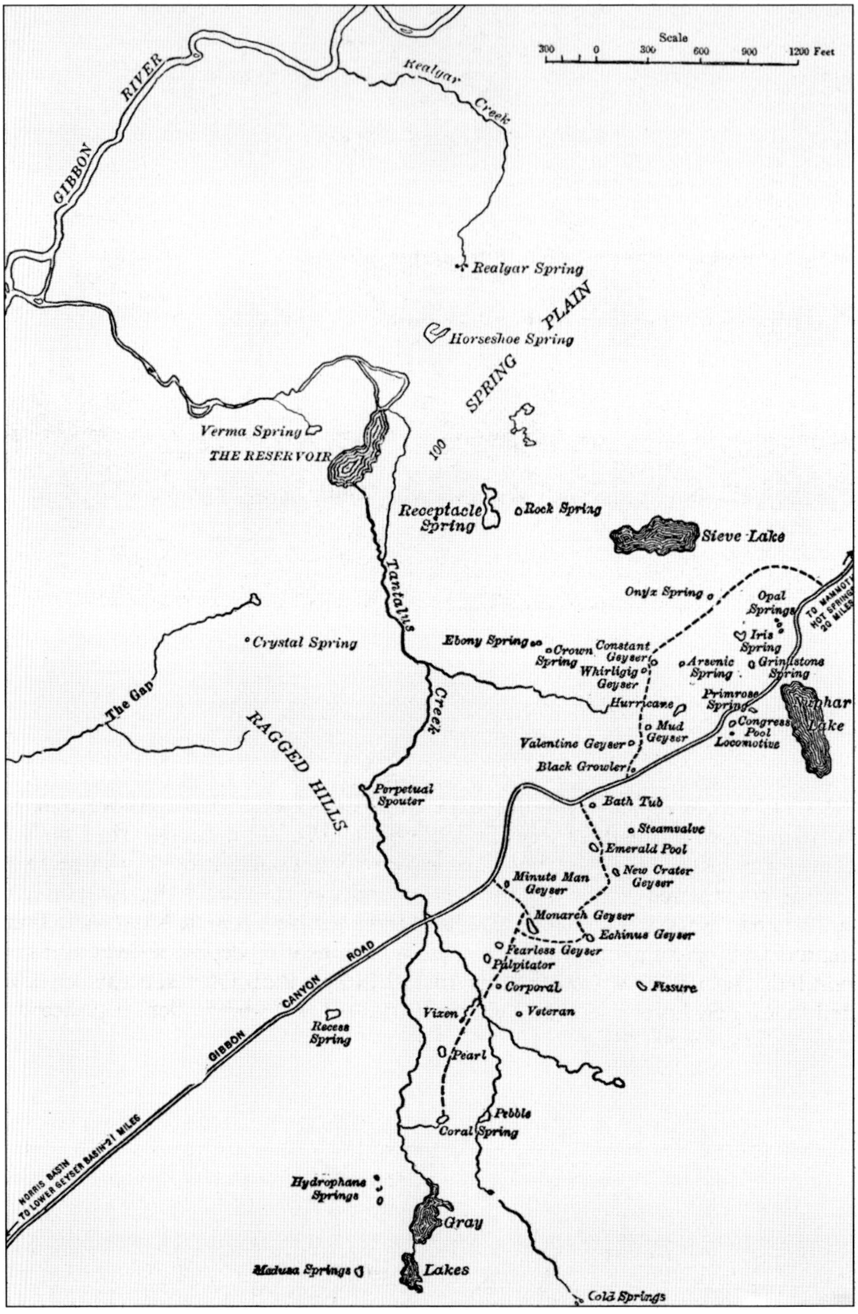

This map, from the 1929 *Geysers of the Yellowstone National Park* by Walter Weed, shows many of the features that drew early visitors to see Norris Geyser Basin. One Hundred Spring Plain is at the far north end of the basin. The area roughly north of the road is the Porcelain Basin, and features south of the road are in the Back Basin. Those traveling by stagecoach were often dropped off to walk the trails down into Porcelain Basin and One Hundred Spring Plain and were picked up at "Minute Man Geyser," now called Minute Geyser, where seats and a loading platform were built. Yellowstone opened to automobiles on August 1, 1915, and by 1917, all transportation was motorized. (Weed, 1929.)

By 1883, tents were available to travelers exploring Norris Geyser Basin. Above, a steamy Norris Geyser Basin is seen in this 1915 view. By 1886, Supt. D.W. Wear reported that the Yellowstone Park Association had erected a new hotel, but within a year it was destroyed by fire and a temporary building was constructed. In 1887, acting superintendent Capt. Moses Harris reported that "this is a long and narrow one-story building built of one-inch pine boards. It has some twenty small sleeping rooms, is cold and open with no appliance for heating beyond a sheet iron stove in the common hall." It burned in 1892. Finally, in 1901, Capt. John Pitcher, acting superintendent, reported that a new hotel had been built, as shown below. (Above, Detroit postcard no. 7239, 1915; below, *Wonderland 1902*.)

In 1901, Capt. John Pitcher, the acting superintendent, stated that the location of the Norris Hotel on the terrace above the Porcelain Basin, shown above, "has been built on a far better site than that occupied by the old lunch station, which was some distance from the geyser basin . . . The new hotel is so conveniently located that the visitors can now sit on its broad and sheltered veranda, after having their luncheon, and while awaiting the arrival of their coaches, they will be greatly interested in watching the playing of the geysers in the distance below them; or if they prefer to do so, they can stroll leisurely through the basin and await the arrival of their coaches at the Monarch Geyser, where comfortable seats and a shelter have been provided." The Norris Hotel was also called the Norris Lunch House or Lunch Station, as seen below in a view from 1912. It closed in 1916 and was demolished in 1928. (Above, *1901 Superintendent's Report*; below, Acmegraph postcard no. 6501, 1912.)

Although One Hundred Spring Plain is no longer accessible to visitors, Cinder Pool above is a very interesting pool, covered with "cinders" identified as elemental sulfur that has been colored black by pyrite. Researchers lowered a probe into the pool in 1969 and discovered that a pot of molten sulfur sits at about 65 feet below the surface. Only two other countries in the world have such "pots" of molten sulfur—Japan and New Zealand. Below is the Reservoir, a large thermal pool that collects much of the flow of Tantalus Creek in One Hundred Spring Plain before the creek flows into the Gibbon River. A.C. Peale first identifies the pool in the 1878 *USGGS*: "No. 80 is a large lake-like sulfur pool;" it can be seen on the map from 1929 shown on page 28. (Photographs by the authors when access was permitted by special request from the National Park Service, 1999.)

Visitors, in the past as well as today, often began their journey following a boardwalk out into Porcelain Basin. This trail leaves currently from the Norris Museum. Half of the 1904 stereograph at left is captioned "Looking down past the 'Black Growler' and 'Boiler' Steam Vents to Constant Geyser." Black Growler, shown below, has had as many as five vents. All are in an alcove eroded by Valentine Geyser. Temperatures have ranged from close to boiling to the highest recorded surface temperature in Yellowstone—just over 280 degrees Fahrenheit. (Left, YNPMC, YELL #131037; below, USGS, dce00165, C.E. Dobbin, 1924.)

Both photographs show Constant Geyser in eruption, a favorite of early visitors. Of 84 notable features at Norris listed in the 1988 *USGS Paper 1456*, seventy have erupted as geysers. Although observers such as Arnold Hague, appointed geologist in Yellowstone in 1883, remarked on Constant Geyser's regularity, this geyser has seasons of frequent activity as well as seasons of complete inactivity. In recent years, it has erupted to about 20 to 30 feet with intervals of minutes to hours. Nearby are Whirligig and Little Whirligig Geysers. Currently, Whirligig is active with intervals of several hours, whereas Little Whirligig is inactive. Out in the flats beyond Constant Geyser, the Arsenic, Fireball, and Pinto Geysers may surprise the observer as they walk the Porcelain Basin boardwalk. (Above, Detroit postcard no. 12045, 1902; right, AandD.)

Many geysers in the Porcelain Basin are quite irregular, ranging from dormant to frequent in their patterns, with little understanding of their variability compared to geysers in other basins. This photograph shows Whirligig Geyser (left) and Constant Geyser (right) in a dual eruption. Others geysers nearby that might be seen in the Porcelain Basin include Arsenic, Fireball, and Blue Geysers. (Courtesy of Graham Meech.)

The Carnegie II drill hole, drilled in 1929, is located above the Porcelain Basin and behind Congress Pool. According to Allen and Day, the hole was drilled down to 265 feet, with measured temperatures of over 400 degrees Fahrenheit and pressures of 300 pounds per square inch. Superheated jets of steam escaped the ground nearby, so the drillers poured five tons of cement into the drill hole to stabilize it. (AandD.)

This 1967 photograph shows Dr. A. Steiner, a New Zealand petrologist, with an unidentified woman standing next to the Carnegie II drill hole. The concrete plug and rocks used to stabilize the drill hole are shown. Shortly after this photograph was taken, another drill hole was completed over 400 feet away. Later, steam and hot water broke out near the Carnegie II drill hole. (USGS, wde00034, Donald E. White, 1967.)

Stagecoach travelers, as well as motorized travelers in later years, visited "Devil's Ink Well" as they continued south on the Grand Loop Road while heading to the Back Basin. The road was rerouted away from the Norris Geyser Basin by early 1968. This spring carried many names, including "Devil's Ink Stand," "Devil's Ink Pot," and "Devil's Bathtub"; it is now named Bathtub Spring. (YNPMC, YELL #131036.)

Bathtub Spring has a history of geyser activity, as the photograph above illustrates. However, the main attraction as travelers headed south was "Minute Man Geyser" (shown below), now called Minute Geyser. It erupted regularly to 60 feet through at least the 1930s and was so popular that stands and tents were erected to shelter and transport visitors. The geyser was close to the road until early 1968, when the road was relocated. Sadly, prior to the relocation the geyser was subjected to vandals who filled the vent full of rocks. It currently acts as a perpetual spouter from a few inches to a foot or so high. (Above, LOC, 3b00407u; below, YNPMC, YELL #134836.)

Minute Geyser has two vents (shown at right). The northwestern vent produced the larger eruptions, measured to 65 feet high in this photograph from 1947, when both vents were unobstructed. An inspection in 1969 indicated that vandals had filled the northwestern vent with rocks, and only the southeast vent continues to show minor activity. Automobiles were allowed in the park on August 1, 1915, and horse-drawn vehicles were prohibited in 1917. In the photograph below, from 1917, the Minute Geyser's stands, designed for stagecoach passengers, have not yet been removed. (Right, AandD; below, YNPMC, YELL #541, 1917.)

From its first observed eruption in 1881 until 1913, Monarch Geyser (above) was the second-largest geyser ever to erupt in Norris Geyser Basin. According to the 1988 *USGS Paper 1456*, "a massive column of water would rocket to a height estimated at 25 to 40 meters [82 to 131 feet], with one observer claiming 60 meters [nearly 200 feet]." It is likely that the violence of its eruptions damaged its subsurface channels, as it is now a quiet discharging pool (seen below). (Above, AandD; below, photograph by the authors, 2012.)

Vixen Geyser is a small but enjoyable geyser. As shown above in an 1889 woodcut, early visitors were interested in it. According to the 1988 *USGS Paper 1456*, "[Park Historian] Lee Whittlesey . . . found obscure records in the National Archives indicating that Superintendent Norris supervised the removal of Vixen's natural one-meter-high cone and shipped it as a unique specimen to the U.S. National Museum. No direct confirming evidence . . . remains except, possibly, the unnatural-looking nearly square vent and a surrounding iron-stained zone." A major eruption of Vixen Geyser is seen at right; it can also have smaller minor eruptions. (Above, Riley, 1889; right, courtesy of Pat Snyder.)

Porkchop Geyser demonstrates the variability of the Norris Geyser Basin features. Allen and Day in the 1920s and 1930s and D.E. White in the 1950s studied this spring because of the chemical composition of its waters. Until 1985, it was a clear, opalescent blue pool with some discharge and an occasional eruption that emptied the pool (above). In 1985, it became a continuous spouter with a roar that visitors could hear at the Norris Museum 660 yards away (left). Then, on September 5, 1989, Porkchop Geyser exploded. Rocks surrounding the old vent were tilted up; some were thrown more than 216 feet away. Now, it is again a clear, opalescent blue pool without eruptive activity (below). (Above, USGS, wde00009, Donald E. White, 1972; left and below, photographs by the authors, 1985 and 2005.)

In the 1878 USGGS, Echinus Geyser was named by Dr. Peale, thinking the pebbles resembled a spine-covered sea urchin. He saw an eruption, but until 1948 it was an irregular performer. For 50 years, from 1948 to 1998, it typically erupted 40–60 feet high every 35–75 minutes, as seen above in this 1988 photograph. Beginning in 1998, Echinus had longer and longer periods of dormancy, with infrequent eruptions. The last two eruptions were on June 18, 2012, and May 05, 2013. According to the 1988 *USGS Paper 1456*, "Spinose red, yellow and brown sinter is characteristic of acid waters, consistent with the recorded pH of 3.35 to 3.5." Acid geysers are extremely rare. Most of the world's acid geysers are found at Norris Geyser Basin. Echinus is now generally a quiet overflowing pool, as shown below in this 2012 photograph. It features the same coloration and spiny sinter previously observed. (Photographs by the authors, above, 1988, below, 2012.)

In 1878, Steamboat Geyser (above) broke through the side of a hill. First, it was a roaring steam vent, and then it became a geyser. Steamboat had a few large eruptions over the next 40-plus years, with an eruption in 1911 described as reaching about 250 feet. The geyser waited 50 years before erupting again in 1961. In the 1960s, Steamboat had over 100 major eruptions, with some reaching nearly 400 feet high (left). Only three eruptions were reported in the 1970s. From 1982 to 1985, Steamboat had 40 more major eruptions. The most recent eruption was July 31, 2013, after a hiatus of over eight years. The eruption consists of a water phase for up to 20 minutes followed by a steam phase that lasts many hours. (Above, Weed, 1929; left, YNPDSF, 05364, Richard Lake, 1966.)

Four

Lower Geyser Basin

The Lower Geyser Basin is the largest basin in the park, studied extensively by Dr. Hayden in his Yellowstone surveys in the 1870s. Allen and Day estimated the total area at 15 square miles, with a thermal discharge of 24 cubic feet of water per second, greater than any other basin in Yellowstone. The central area of this basin is level and covered with deposits, meadowlands, and few trees. The 600 hot springs, geysers, and mud pots in the area are divided into 21 groups. The groups in this basin accessible by roads and trails are those along Firehole Lake Drive, including Great Fountain, White Dome, Pink Cone, and Black Warrior Groups; those in the Fountain Group; and those in the Kaleidoscope and Sprinkler Groups, visible but not accessible from the Fountain Boardwalk. North and east of the Fountain Group are the Thud and Quagmire Groups, also visible from the road but currently not accessible, and those in the Morning Mist and Culex Basin Groups, along the Mary Mountain Trail. This trail traverses the Central Plateau and Hayden Valley, ending south of the Upper and Lower Falls. It approximates the trail taken by most of the early explorers who entered Yellowstone, visited Mud Volcano and Yellowstone Lake, and then crossed to see the geyser basins of the Firehole River. Finally, west of the Fountain Group and along the Fountain Flats Road are the Marshall Hotel, River, Sentinel Meadows, Fairy Meadows, Fairy Creek, and Imperial Groups. In the early days of the park, the features that became significant tourist attractions included Fountain Geyser, Fountain Paint Pot (originally called the "Mammoth Paint Pots"), Great Fountain Geyser, and Imperial Geyser.

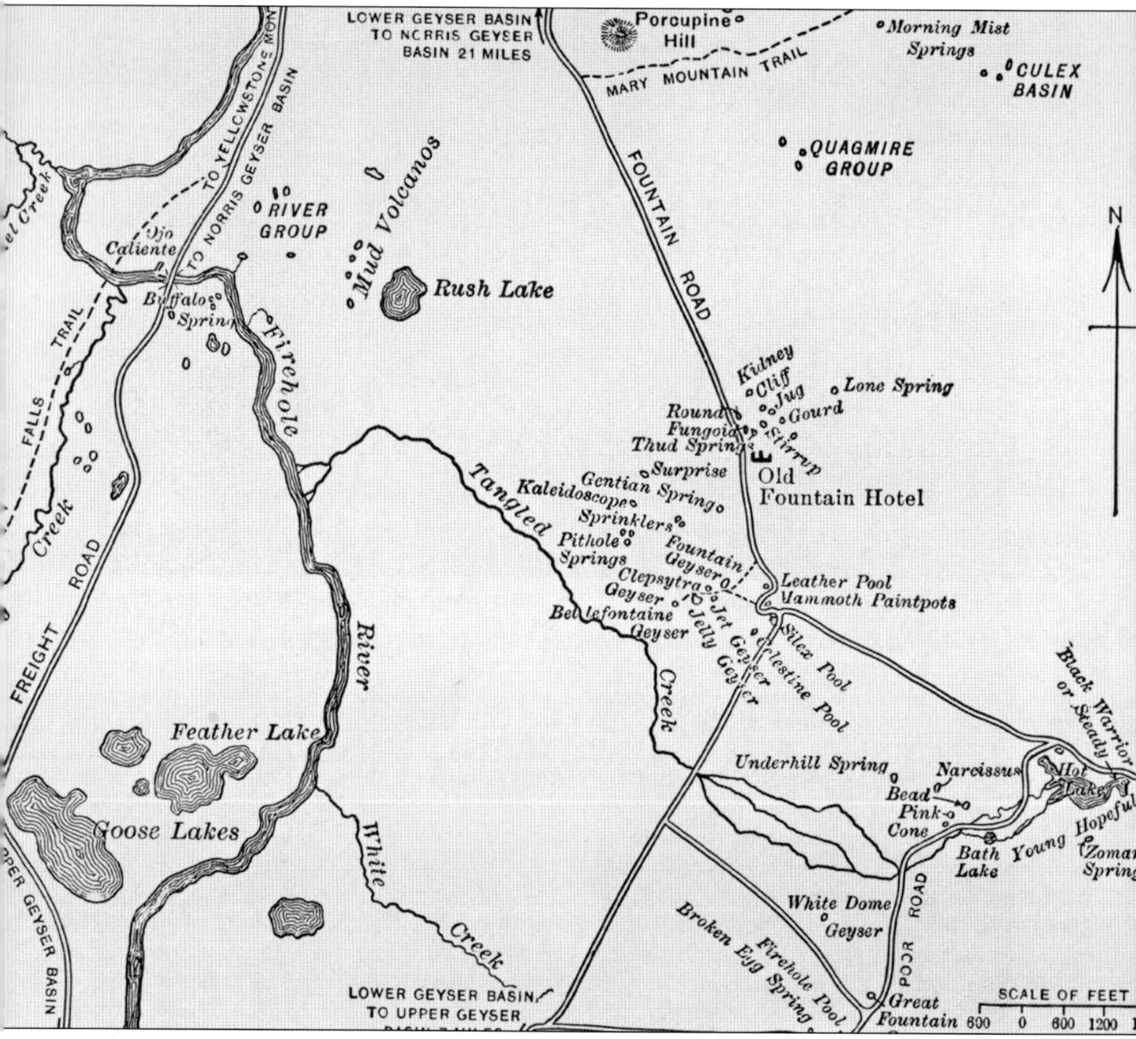

This 1929 map of the Lower Geyser Basin shows the "Fountain Road," part of the Grand Loop Road. The "Fountain Road" went past the Old Fountain Hotel site, between Leather Pool and "Mammoth Paint Pots," now named Fountain Paint Pot. It returned between the Fountain Paint Pot and "Silex Pool," now called Silex Spring. Today's road no longer loops around "Mammoth Paint Pots." The Grand Loop Road has been rerouted east of the Fountain Paint Pot. The roads that go to Black Warrior Springs, Pink Cone, White Dome, and Great Fountain Geysers have also been rerouted. The "Old Freight Road" is now called Fountain Flats Road. Today, it ends for vehicle traffic north of Ojo Caliente Spring, but it remains both a hiking and a biking trail to the Sentinel Meadows Group, River Group, Fairy Falls Group, and Imperial Group, ending at the parking lot south of Midway Geyser Basin. (Weed, 1929.)

George W. Marshall built the Marshall Hotel, the second hotel built in Yellowstone. According to acting superintendent Capt. Moses Harris, he was granted a lease to build the hotel in 1884. By 1888, Harris called the accommodations "entirely inadequate . . . a two-story log building, has been supplemented by two cheap wooden structures two-stories high . . . the partitions . . . are so thin as to afford but little privacy." (BYALE, 1066003, T.W. Ingersoll, c. 1885.)

Nonetheless, the Marshall Hotel served visitors until the Fountain Hotel (pictured) was opened in 1891. According to Capt. George S. Anderson, acting superintendent, "The old hotel at the Lower Basin was vacated . . . and the new building at the Fountain was then occupied. It is the largest, best built and in every way the finest building in the Park." (Acmegraph postcard no. 6514, 1912.)

Visitors spent two nights at the Fountain Hotel, first visiting the features near the hotel, and then exploring the Upper Geyser Basin. A pipeline shown here, still visible today, carried hot water from Leather Pool in the foreground to provide for the guests at the hotel. Once automobiles entered the park in 1915, travel times shortened; the hotel was abandoned in 1917 and torn down in 1927. (YNPDSF, 02772.)

In this view, Thud Group is shown in the field behind the trees where the Fountain Hotel stood. This area received much attention from visitors and workers at the hotel. Some of that attention was in the form of dumping garbage into features such as nearby Thud Spring. The photograph shows Thud Geyser, which made a thud- like sound when erupting, as described by visitors in the late 1800s. (1878 *USGGS*.)

In 1897, Fountain Geyser eruptions could be seen from the Fountain Hotel, but the steam on the hotel side often blocked the view. Fountain Geyser's pool is shown filled in this view, prior to an eruption, with the Fountain Hotel in the background. In the early park days, this geyser was very regular, becoming a visitor favorite. (Acmegraph postcard no. 6493.)

Fountain Geyser was best seen in eruption from close up, and a footpath could be followed to the geyser. In the late 1800s, the geyser erupted every four to six hours from a rather square crater, 20 by 39 feet in size. North of the geyser was a pool that received the overflow from Fountain's eruptions. In the early years, this pool gave no indication of its eruptive power. (Weed, 1929.)

Visitors usually began their explorations with the Fountain Group near the Fountain Hotel. A 1912 Haynes Guide indicates that Fountain Geyser ceased eruptions in July 1899, and that an immense geyser broke out nearby in a pool north of the Fountain Geyser; this geyser is now called Morning Geyser. Morning Geyser, seen at left, is still one of the most powerful geysers in Yellowstone. When it formed, eruptions were loud and ejected geyserite up to 200 feet. Soon, Fountain Geyser returned to activity, but its eruptions were more irregular, becoming rare from 1911 until 1947. Now, Morning Geyser is noted for powerful eruptions that make thumping sounds and occasionally discharge small rocks, but Fountain Geyser is a more frequent player, often erupting twice a day. The photograph below, taken on July 4, 1991, shows the first known instance of both geysers erupting together since the 1959 Hebgen Lake earthquake. (Left, YNPDSF, 05147, George Marler, 1959; below, photograph by the authors, 1991.)

The center of this William Henry Jackson photograph shows the crater of Fountain Geyser with a horse standing in the background. This image was taken during the 1872 government survey of Yellowstone. Jackson took this photograph while standing near the channel where water flows out of Fountain's crater towards Morning Geyser's crater. (USGS, 01567, 1872.)

Massive eruptions from Morning Geyser in 1959 demonstrate the power of this geyser. The back edge of Fountain's crater can be seen where the geyserite channel allows water to enter. Dr. Peale described this pool in 1878 as part of nearby Fountain Geyser, saying it was not known to erupt. (YNPDSF, 05148.)

In the late 1890s, Spasm Geyser was known to erupt to 30 feet. The crater has changed due to a steam explosion, and so have its eruptions. This geyser was named "Jet" by members of the USGGS in 1872. The name was later changed to Spasm, and a nearby feature was named Jet instead. (YNPDSF, 05149, George Marler, 1959.)

The early explorers described Clepsydra Geyser as a very regular geyser, erupting every three minutes, "Like the ancient water clock of that name, it marks the passage of time by the discharge of water." It is a member of the Fountain Group that was strongly affected by the 1959 Hebgen Lake earthquake. Since the earthquake, Clepsydra erupts nearly continuously, occasionally stopping after a Fountain eruption. (YNPDSF, 05112, George Marler, 1960.)

Jelly Geyser erupts in the foreground with possibly New Bellefontaine Geyser on the left and Clepsydra Geyser on the right in the background. Jelly has one of the larger craters in the Fountain Group at about 30 feet by 16 feet. The main crater of Jelly shows unmistakable evidence of explosive origin. In 1878, Dr. Peale described it as erupting to three feet. (YNPDSF, 05110, S. Canter, 1965.)

Fountain Paint Pot has been a visitor favorite since the early days. The "Mud Puffs" are described as being 40 by 60 feet in size with 30 to 40 mud cones in the 1878 *USGGS*. Later, Allen and Day indicate that they are 90 by 120 feet in size. Wooden railings that protect the visitor from splashing mud can be seen in this photograph. (USGS, lwt02084, W.T. Lee.)

Along Firehole Lake Drive, Great Fountain Geyser was a main attraction for the early park visitors, located only two miles south of the Fountain Hotel. Great Fountain Geyser is seen sizzling in this view while a park ranger looks on. (AandD.)

William Henry Jackson took this photograph of Great Fountain Geyser. Jackson was invited by Dr. Hayden to accompany both the 1871 and the 1872 USGGS. His photographs, along with reports from the USGGS, played a role in influencing Congress in 1872 to establish Yellowstone National Park. (Detroit chromolithograph, 1902.)

George Marler was a ranger-naturalist for decades, starting in 1931. Marler's study of and extensive notes on Yellowstone geysers documented changes in geyser behavior over time. He made many contributions to the field of hydrothermal geology at Yellowstone National Park. Great Fountain Geyser erupts in this 1959 view. (YNPDSF, 04825, George Marler, 1959.)

Great Fountain Geyser (pictured), surrounded by a 150-foot circular platform, can erupt from 75 to 200 feet in height for over 35 minutes. In 1871, Dr. Hayden observed an eruption of the geyser and named it "Architectural Geyser." According to Whittlesey in *Yellowstone Place Names*, early visitors found it difficult to visit the geyser because of the lack of good roads. (AandD.)

White Dome Geyser (pictured) was named by members of the 1871 USGGS. The geyser has one of the largest sinter cones in Yellowstone Park. Allen and Day describe the cone as being 65 by 90 feet at the base and rising 12 feet in height. In 1929, eruptions were measured up to 29 feet above the cone. (1878 *USGGS*, William Henry Jackson.)

White Dome Geyser is shown in eruption. The size of the cone indicates the White Dome is one of the oldest geysers in Yellowstone. The geyser is located in an open area with small thermal features nearby. Deposits of sinter have nearly sealed the vent's opening. (YNPDSF, 05451, George Marler).

Jim Peaco, the park photographer, took this photograph from a bucket truck, showing White Dome's vent. According to Marler, "The large size of White Dome's cone, plus the fact that its pipe is approaching the sealing-in stage due to the internal accretion of sinter, is indicative that hot-spring activity has been occurring at this site for what would seem to be a few thousand years." (YNPDSF, 17857, Jim Peaco, 2003.)

Allen and Day took this photograph of Pink Cone in 1930. They write, "The Pink Cone is a small, hollow, truncated cone; its dimensions being according to Peale, 18 inches in height, 5 feet in breath, and 2 feet inside diameter at the orifice. The silica has a reddish tone, possibly due to manganese which it contains in small amounts." (AandD.)

This photograph from 1959 shows an eruption of Pink Cone Geyser. The geyser can reach heights of 15 to 20 feet. Eruptions are known from the late 1880s. According to T. Scott Bryan in *The Geysers of Yellowstone,* the 1959 Hebgen Lake earthquake increased Pink Cone's activity, and for 10 days after the geyser erupted almost constantly. (YNPDSF, 05153, George Marler, 1959.)

In 1871, Dr. Hayden named Steady Geyser, within Firehole Lake. Steady Geyser is a perpetual spouter, erupting continuously with two separate jets issuing from a low sinter mound. Allen and Day estimated the height of the eruption as between 15 and 30 feet, and it was considered the largest perpetual spouter in Yellowstone. Currently, it only erupts to about three feet. (AandD.)

Dr. Peale, while on the 1878 USGGS, discovered a group of springs along a long fissure in the area of Earthquake Geyser. The 7.3-magnitude 1959 Hebgen Lake earthquake, which affected many geysers in Yellowstone, caused one of these features to erupt. Marler saw one of these eruptions, similar to one shown in the photograph. He stated, "This spring was given the name Earthquake Geyser due to its spectacular performance resulting from the 1959 earthquake. There is no record of previous eruptive activity." As reported by Marler, eruptions reached heights of 100 feet, and it emitted large quantities of water. However, these large eruptions ceased after a few days. After a steam vent formed nearby, Earthquake Geyser became a perpetual spouter due to the loss of energy from this vent. (YNPDSF, 05142, Lewis, 1959.)

Mound Geyser, in the River Group, was named in 1878. The geyser is on a large mound, and water from eruptions flows into an intricately formed runoff channel into the Firehole River. Researchers Allen and Day measured a water temperature of over 233 degrees at 36 feet deep. (AandD.)

Conch Spring, also known as Fortress Geyser, is also in the River Group. It was named by members of the 1871 USGGS. In the 1870s it was known to erupt to about five feet. The geyser has an impressive formation and black coloration in its runoff channel. (1878 *USGGS*, William Henry Jackson.)

Part of the Imperial Group of the Lower Geyser Basin, Imperial Geyser first erupted in 1927. In August 1927, Ranger Summerland and Allen saw Imperial Geyser erupting to less than 25 feet high from a crater 75 feet in diameter and 2 to 6 feet high. The next year it was seen again, but it was more powerful, with heights from 50 to 80 feet measured by Allen and Day. (AandD.)

This 1928 photograph shows the wall and fissure from which Imperial Geyser erupted. Allen and Day measured the depth to 74 feet, with a temperature at this depth of 212 degrees Fahrenheit. During its eruptions in the late 1920s, great quantities of water were discharged. Imperial went dormant in October 1929. This dormancy lasted for 37 years, according to Marler. (AandD.)

Allen and Day noted in 1928 and 1929 that Imperial Geyser eruptions "began with marked suddenness and ended with equal abruptness . . . As a rule [one] or two eruptions were said to occur within a period of about 24 hours." After an inactive period, however, it rejuvenated in 1966, and eruptions were smaller and on the side of the pool. (YNPDSF, 11048, R Robinson, 1974.)

Spray Geyser, also in the Imperial Group, is about quarter of a mile from Imperial Geyser. Marler suspected that the energy for this geyser might be from preglacial springs now buried under Twin Butte, with the present spring representing a new outlet. The water from Spray erupts through glacial boulders. (YNPDSF, 05145, 1967.)

This photograph from the Sentinel Meadow Group, probably by William Henry Jackson, shows Flat Cone in the foreground and Steep Cone in the background. Both were named by members of the 1872 USGGS. Steep Cone is larger and higher that Flat Cone. A boggy marsh often separates the two, making the hike between them difficult. In the late 1880s, people began to visit these areas. (1878 *USGGS*.)

Iron Pot is also in the Sentinel Meadow Group. The crater is about 16 feet across and 14–16 feet deep. In this photograph, water is seen rising in the iron-colored bowl prior to an eruption. An eruption begins suddenly, doming up to six feet above the surface for 25 minutes, but Iron Pot never overflows. (Photograph by the authors, 2006.)

In 1872, the USGGS team discovered a hot spring in Sentinel Meadow, which it named Red Terrace Spring. In 1880, Superintendent Norris named the spring Queen's Laundry because he saw men bathing in the pool and washing their clothes, according to Lee Whittlesey in *Yellowstone Place Names*. In 1881, Superintendent Norris began to build a bathhouse, still standing unfinished today. (YNPDSF, 02795.)

Kaleidoscope Geyser, in the Kaleidoscope Group, lies northwest of Fountain Geyser. Fountain Hotel visitors had access to this area from now closed roads. Marler said, "An eruption of Kaleidoscope is a spectacular sight . . . the frequency of the activity . . . with the fact that it plays to a height of 35 to 40 feet, make it most interesting to observe." (Courtesy of Graham Meech, 2006.)

Five

Midway Geyser Basin

Midway Geyser Basin was first named the Half-Way Group by members of the 1871 USGGS and was later named Egeria Springs by Dr. Peale in the 1878 *USGGS*, but in many reports it is called "Hell's Half Acre," or simply the "Great Hot Springs." According to Dr. Peale in the 1878 *USGGS*, "The springs occupy an area extending along the river about a mile in length and a quarter mile in width . . . on a mound about 50 feet above the river level." The basin has two remarkable springs, one with a history of an immense display of thermal energy—Excelsior Geyser—and one that excels in size and beauty—Grand Prismatic Spring. The main basin is about a mile south of the Firehole Lake Drive southern entrance and about five and a half miles north of the exit for the Upper Geyser Basin. Dr. Peale, in the 1878 *USGGS*, enumerates 39 springs, but Allen and Day indicate only 30 that are significant, with five having superheated waters and four exhibiting geyser activity. According to Scott Bryan in *Geysers of Yellowstone*, 20 features have shown geyser activity. Of the geysers, only two are on today's boardwalk; the remaining geysers are in small areas without boardwalks and include the Rabbit Creek and Flood Groups.

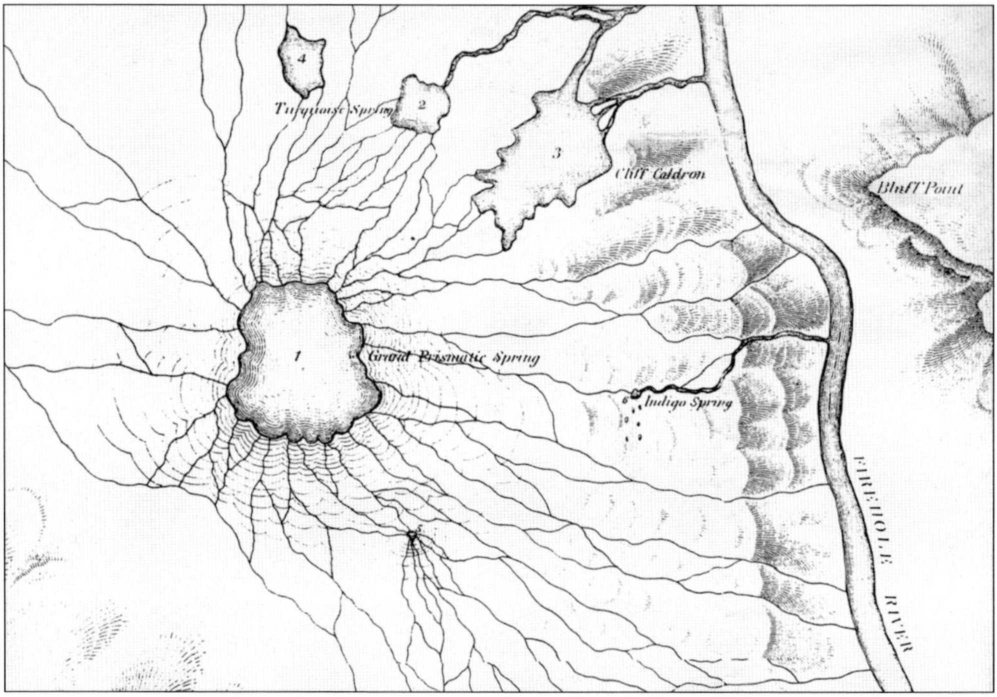

According to William Henry Jackson, "'Great Hot Springs' [are] midway between the Upper and Lower Basins of the Firehole River and on the west side. A vast accumulation of siliceous matter, built up 50 feet above the river, upon the summit of which are three large boiling springs." The map above, from 1878, shows four springs. The largest spring (1) is named Grand Prismatic Spring; 2 is Turquoise Spring; 3 is "Cliff Cauldron" or Excelsior Geyser; and 4 is now named Opal Pool. The *1909 Campbell Guide* describes the stagecoaches stopping at a platform from which stairs lead down to a footbridge across the Firehole River. The painting *The Great Blue Spring of the Lower Geyser Basin, Yellowstone* by Thomas Moran (below) shows "Cliff Cauldron," or today's Excelsior Geyser. (Both, 1878 *USGGS*.)

A fur trapper, Osborne Russell, wrote the first known description of Grand Prismatic Spring (depicted above and below): "At length we came to a boiling Lake about 300 feet in diameter . . . The steam which arose from it was of three distinct Colors." This parallels the description in the 1878 *USGGS*: "Over the central pit or bowl, which is constantly boiling and sending up vast columns of steam, the color is a deep blue, which fades into green towards the edge. The surrounding shallower basin has a yellow tint fading into orange, and outside the rim is a brilliant red deposit. This fades into purples, browns and grays, the whole being on the gray-white ground." Grand Prismatic Spring is the largest hot spring, at 250 by 380 feet in size, in Yellowstone and is considered the third-largest in the world. (Above, 1878 *USGGS*, William Henry Jackson; below, photograph by authors, 2005.)

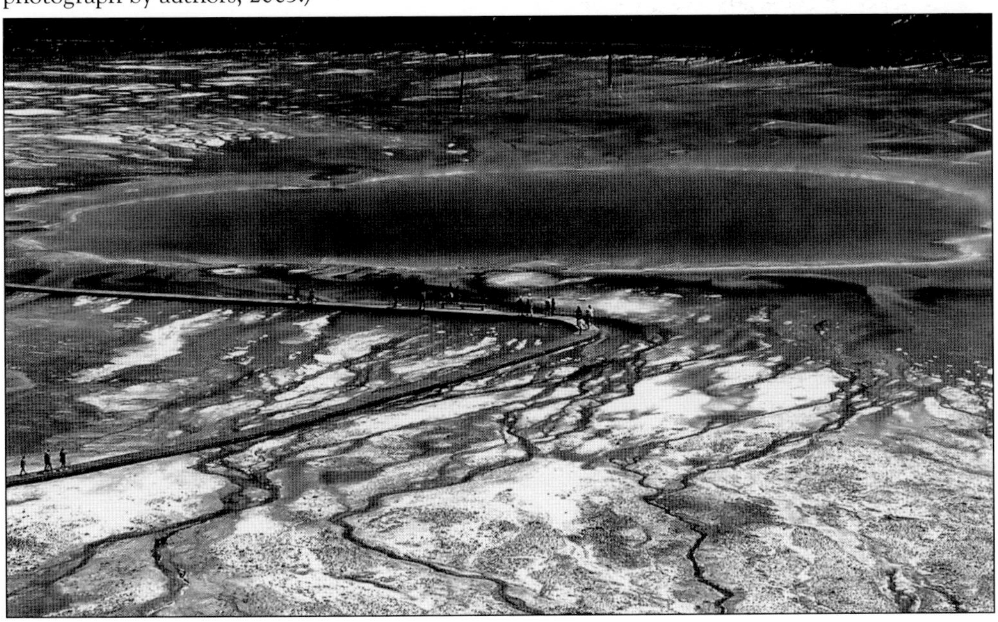

Dr. Peale named Turquoise Pool in the 1878 *USGGS*: "This is a deep, blue tinted, square spring, measuring 100 feet by 100 feet . . . The color is intense in hue." It is a cool pool, only 50–60 degrees Fahrenheit, but it shows a relationship to Excelsior, having dropped far below overflow when Excelsior Geyser was active. Turquoise Pool also dropped after the 1959 Hebgen Lake earthquake, as shown in the photograph above, perhaps looking as it did when Excelsior erupted. After draining following the earthquake, it refilled, as shown below in this 1960 photograph. (Above, YNPDSF, 06178, Lewis; below, YNPDSF, 06179.)

Opal Pool, shown above, is "Spring 4" in the 1878 *USGGS*. According to Marler, prior to the eruptions of 1947, Opal was not suspected as being a geyser. It has had rare, brief eruptions in the years since then. According to Marler, "Previous to an eruption of Opal there is greatly increased overflow. The temperature approaches the boiling point . . . The water over the main crater undergoes a great bulge. It becomes dome-like, the center being 4 to 5 feet above the former surface. The bulging is fleeting. Almost simultaneously an explosion occurs [shown below], which sends up several rockets of water. During an eruption one or more bursts have been noted to rise to a height of about 50 feet. Following an eruption the crater fills slowly." (Photographs by the authors, 1993.)

Excelsior Geyser is an immense crater on the Firehole River (left) that is 328 by 276 feet in size. The surface of the water is deep blue and is 15–20 feet below the rim. When first observed by the USGGS team, it was not thought to be a geyser and was named "Cliff Cauldron." In 1881, however, Superintendent Norris saw huge eruptions and found them to be "so immeasurably excelling any other geyser, ancient or modern, known to history, that I find but one name fitting, and herein christen it the 'Excelsior.'" According to Norris, "During much of the summer the eruptions were simply incredible, elevating to heights of 100 to 300 feet sufficient water to render the rapid Firehole River, nearly 100 yards wide, a torrent of steaming hot water, and hurling rocks of from one to 100 pounds weight . . . over the surrounding acres." An eruption is shown in the woodcut below. (Left, YNPMC, YELL #128454 from 1901; below, Riley, 1889.)

EXCELSIOR GEYSER, ERUPTING 400 FEET HIGH. DIAMETER OF CRATER ABOUT 50 X 150.

Six

Upper Geyser Basin

A fur trapper, Warren Angus Ferris, gave an early account of his visit to the Upper Geyser Basin in 1834. His writings were first published as serial stories in the 1840s, then edited and compiled later into *Life in the Rocky Mountains*, published in 1983. He describes "the largest of these wonderful fountains, projects a column of boiling water several feet in diameter, to the height of more than 150 feet."

Members of the Washburn Expedition explored the Upper Geyser Basin in 1870. Others visited this area before the Washburn Expedition, such as Native Americans and hunters. The expedition spent a short time in the Upper Basin and saw one geyser erupt several times. As a result, the expedition members named it Old Faithful Geyser. They also saw other geysers erupt and named them—including Grand, Beehive, Giantess, Castle, and Giant Geysers. When they returned from the trip, their reports, magazine articles, and speeches encouraged the federal government to fund the first US Geological and Geographical Survey to the area in the summer of 1871, led by Ferdinand V. Hayden. Dr. Hayden took a number of scientists and support people into the area and produced reports, maps, paintings, and photographs. The photographer who traveled with the survey and documented many of the Yellowstone wonders was William Henry Jackson. Dr. Hayden returned to Yellowstone and surrounding areas with another government survey party in 1872 and 1878. The detailed maps and descriptions from his survey in 1871 influenced the decision to create America's first national park in 1872.

The Upper Geyser Basin is comprised of several geyser groups, including the Old Faithful, Geyser Hill, Castle, Grand, Giant, Daisy, Grotto, Morning Glory, Cascade, Biscuit Basin, Black Sand Basin, Myriad, and Pipeline Meadows Groups.

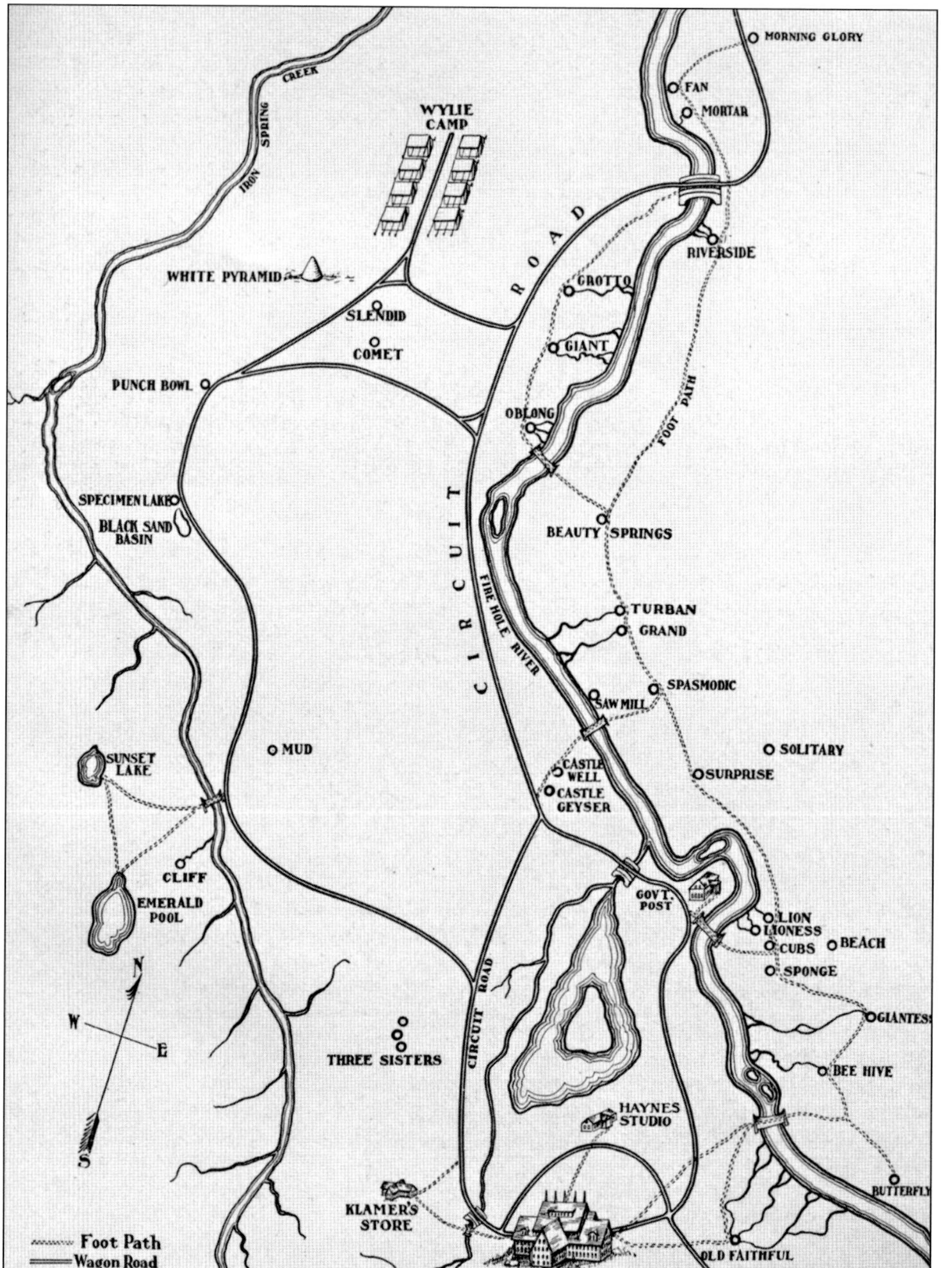

This map from the *1909 Campbell's New Revised Complete Guide* shows the Upper Geyser Basin. It shows the original Grand Loop Road ("Circuit Road"), along with the historic locations for the Wylie Tourist Camp, the old government post, the Klamer's Store (now the Old Faithful Lower Store), and the Haynes Studio, refurbished and reopened as a museum in 2013. To move traffic away from the thermal features, Grand Loop Road was rerouted in 1971–1972, closer to but east of the Iron Spring Creek near Cliff Geyser, Emerald Pool, and Sunset Lake. The "Circuit Road" is now the asphalt hiking and biking path to Morning Glory Pool, and the trails on the east side of the Firehole River are now boardwalks. Most of the famous geysers are identified along with footpaths and old wooden bridges crossing the Firehole River. (Campbell, 1909.)

Shown in the photograph is the Yellowstone National Park Improvement Company camp at the Upper Geyser Basin. This was the park's first tent camp and was in use only from 1883 to 1885. A wooden board was used as a footbridge to span the Firehole River between the Camp and Beehive Geyser. Three men are looking at Beehive Geyser. No boardwalks existed in the early years of the park. (YNPMC, YELL #313, 1883.)

According to the *1887 Superintendent's Report*, "in November 1884 Mr. Carroll T. Hobart entered into an agreement . . . for the construction of a hotel building at the Upper Geyser Basin." This 1889 photograph shows this first hotel at the Upper Geyser Basin, a two-story frame building called the Shack. The hotel was built in 1885 and was destroyed by fire in 1894. (YNPDSF, 02806.)

Visitors are shown on the porch of the building that replaced the Shack after it burned in 1894. The *1895 Superintendent's Report* indicates the old hotel was "replaced by a temporary structure better adapted than was the old one for the purposes of a lunch station but without the means of accommodating visitors over night." Planning began in 1901 for the Old Faithful Inn. (Courtesy of David Monteith.)

This 1905 view of the Old Faithful Inn, opened in 1904, shows the inn with Old Faithful Geyser in eruption. Asymmetrically designed by architect Robert Reamer, "to reflect the chaos of nature," the log hotel was 700 feet long and seven stories high, with an 85-foot-high lobby ceiling. The east and west wings were added in 1913 and 1927, respectively. (*Wonderland 1905*.)

By 1906, a Wylie Camp had been built on the hillside between Daisy Geyser and Grotto Geyser. In this view, the visitors are waiting for their stagecoaches to continue their travels around the park. This camp was abandoned when the Wylie and the Shaw and Powell Camping Companies merged in 1917. (Acmegraph postcard no. 9476, 1912.)

Shaw and Powell Camping Company opened its tent camps in 1898, received a permanent camping assignment in 1913, and by 1914 "completed a bungalow of logs for dining room and lobby at Old faithful camp and piped fine mountain water about 900 feet into that camp," according to the *1914 Superintendent's Report*. This camp eventually became the Old Faithful Lodge. (YNPDSF, 02784, Haynes, 1917.)

More visitor facilities were built in the Upper Geyser Basin to accommodate the influx of travelers. This photograph from 1921 shows the Old Faithful Inn to the left, the swimming pool building to the right with people gathered in front, and Klamer's Store, the roof seen above the swimming pool building. Beehive Geyser's cone is located in the foreground, with an improved bridge across the Firehole River. (YNPDSF, 03028.)

This original swimming pool at Old Faithful was used from 1914 to 1933 and was also called the "Geyser Baths." It was remodeled in 1934, closed in 1948, and dismantled in 1951. Water to heat the swimming pool arrived through a pipe built between the swimming pool and Solitary Geyser on the wooded hill above Geyser Hill. (YNPDSF, 03023.)

The extensive 1934 remodeling of the "Geyser Baths" gave it a new name, "The Plunge at Old Faithful." The hot water from Solitary Geyser, granted to Henry Brothers in 1915, continued to be used until 1948, when the National Park Service revoked his permit and "The Plunge at Old Faithful" was closed. (YNPDSF, 10641.)

Old Faithful Geyser is usually the first destination of visitors to the Upper Geyser Basin. This photograph shows people walking about the cone and platform during an eruption without the safety of today's boardwalks. The image by William Henry Jackson was probably taken during the 1878 USGGS. (USGS, jwh00411.)

This photograph, by William Henry Jackson in the 1870s, of Old Faithful Geyser in eruption shows six individuals standing on the cone. Wind is blowing steam and water away from them. Partially due to the easy access to the geyser, Old Faithful has been heavy damaged over the years. According to Lee Whittlesey in *Yellowstone Place Names*, "this overwhelming tendency of visitors to vandalize in early days was one reason that the U.S. Army took over administration of the Park in 1886." According to Marler, "One of the most interesting examples of a geyser evolving from an earthquake rift is Old Faithful Geyser. Extending across Old Faithful's mound from east to west is a pronounced break in the sinter. The part of the fissure through which Old Faithful issues is but four inches in width. Radiocarbon dating of tree sections entombed in the mound indicates that the earthquake which split it open, permitting the birth of Old Faithful, occurred from 500 to 700 years ago." (USGS, jwh01684.)

Dr. Hayden wrote in 1872, "This is one of the most accommodating geysers in the basin, and during our stay played once an hour quite regularly. On account of this apparent regularity and its position overlooking the valley, Messrs. Langford and Doane called it 'Old Faithful.' It has built up a crater about 20 feet high around its base." The crater is seen in this woodcut. (Riley, 1889.)

Old Faithful's crater was described by Albert B. Guptill in 1897: "This mound is composed of layers of deposit in a succession of distinctly marked terraces which are full of shallow, basin-like pools, the water in which is clear as crystal, and their edges or rims exquisitely beaded and fretted, their bottom showing delicate tints of rose, white saffron, orange, brown and gray." (USGS, jwh00187, William Henry Jackson, 1872.)

This 1888 photograph shows Old Faithful's water column, steam, and water spray, with a visitor standing on the cone. Eruptions were described as starting with a few surges, during which large amounts of water were thrown out, followed by a full eruption of 100–180 feet. All visitors are now prohibited from walking on thermal features to protect both the visitor and the feature. (YNPMC, YELL #119625.)

This winter scene shows Old Faithful Geyser in eruption and the Old Faithful Inn buried under a heavy snowfall. Since 1905, winter keepers have been stationed at the inn to shovel snow off the roof while the inn is closed during the winter months. (Sanford Souvenir Co. postcard no. 1225, 1934.)

This distant elevated view of Old Faithful shows a large group of visitors gathered just outside the spray in 1905. Old Faithful is less than 1,000 feet east and in plain sight of the Old Faithful Inn. After watching Old Faithful erupt, most visitors crossed the Firehole River to Geyser Hill. (BYALE, 1037415, Detroit photograph.)

This 1918 image shows a person standing next to Beehive's cone with the Old Faithful Inn in the background. When Beehive's Indicator—a small geyser near the cone that can erupt before Beehive—was seen from the inn, a bellboy would ring a bell announcing that Beehive Geyser was about to erupt, whereupon tourists would rush out and cross the footbridge to wait for the eruption. (Haynes Real Photo no. 4479.)

This 1887 view shows an eruption of Beehive Geyser from the Old Faithful side of the Firehole River, with visitors standing around watching the large display. A 1910 guide states that a Beehive eruption could reach over 200 feet and last eight minutes. The steaming mound behind and to the right of Beehive is the fountain-type Giantess Geyser. (Haynes, 1887.)

The older, simple plank bridge to Beehive Geyser was rebuilt with a more substantial base and railings. This view shows a 1920s version of the Beehive Bridge with visitors below the cone of Beehive on Geyser Hill. Boardwalks to protect the visitors and the features had not yet been built. (*Haynes Guide*, 1923.)

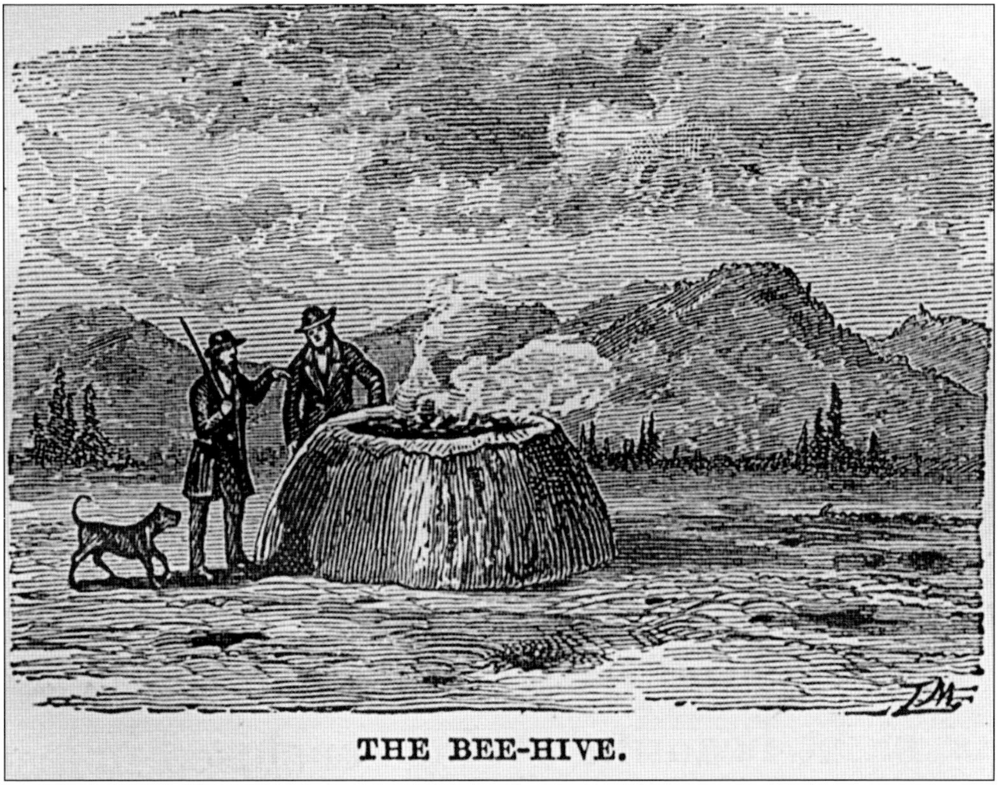

The 1874 illustration above shows an exaggerated Beehive Geyser cone. Like Old Faithful Geyser, Beehive is more powerful early in its eruption, when its maximum height is reached. Water and steam are forced through a narrow opening in the cone and reach from 150 to over 200 feet high, currently lasting for about five minutes. The 1872 view at right shows Beehive's cone. Allen and Day in 1935 stated, "For symmetry and grace no geyser surpasses the Beehive, whether these terms are applied to its cone or its water jet . . . [the cone] at the top, [is] two feet wide at the beginning, narrows rapidly as the depth increases, so that the jet of water is comparatively small." (Above, Richardson, 1874; right, USGS, jwh01575, William Henry Jackson, 1872.)

In 1870, Langford of the Washburn Expedition wrote, "Opposite our camp, on the east side of the Firehole river, is a symmetrical cone resembling an old-fashioned straw beehive with the top cut off. Suddenly, while we were at breakfast this morning, a column of water shot from it, which by quite accurate triangular measurement proved to be 219 feet in height. We named this geyser the 'Bee Hive.'" (YNPDSF, 05039.)

This view from T.W. Ingersoll in 1890 shows Beehive Geyser cone and Castle Geyser across the Firehole River in the background. On the right side is a view of a military post set up near the Firehole River. During these early days, visitors were not restricted to boardwalks and could walk around all the features. Many features were damaged as a result. (BYALE, 1051498.)

In 1902, a military post existed in the meadow across the Firehole River from Geyser Hill. According to T. Scott Bryan in *The Geysers of Yellowstone*, Geyser Hill, with its 50 geysers, is the fourth-largest geyser field in the world. Bears, bison, and elk are sometimes seen on the hill. Microscopic organisms, called cyanobacteria, live in the runoff channels from the springs and geysers. These organisms create the rainbows of color in the channels. The colors of these microscopic organisms, which are a different type and color depending on the temperature of the water in which they live, are good indications of the temperature of the water. Generally, lighter colors of yellows and pinks indicate water up to 167 degrees Fahrenheit. Darker colors of reds and bright oranges indicate temperatures around 140–150 Fahrenheit. The darkest colors of browns and dark greens indicate the cooler waters of 120–140 degrees Fahrenheit. (BYALE, 1037419.)

Giantess Geyser, erupting in this 1887 photograph, is located on the summit of Geyser Hill, which slopes downward to the bank of the Firehole River. The 1870 Washburn Expedition saw this geyser erupt and described a great mass of hot water rushing skyward to 60 feet, with streams of water shooting up further from the crest of this mass to 250 feet. (Haynes, 1887.)

The crater of Giantess Geyser, shown in this 1878 photograph by William Henry Jackson, has been estimated to be about 25 by 35 feet in size and 25 feet deep before narrowing down. An eruption starts with this pool rising up with an outpouring of water. This is followed by the true eruption, which ejects this reservoir of water and can last for days. (1878 *USGGS*.)

This photograph from the 1870s shows a person looking into a nearly full and boiling Teakettle Spring. In 1878, Dr. Peale referred to Teakettle Spring as being an "11 by 7 1/2 feet [in size], 12 feet deep, rim 18 inches high, boiling spring with inky-hued water." Teakettle Spring is west of Giantess before one reaches Sponge Geyser on the boardwalk and can be heard splashing at depth within the crater. (USGS, jwh00659, William Henry Jackson.)

This photograph shows Sponge Geyser with visitors in 1900. Sponge was used by park naturalists as a model to demonstrate the difference between eruptive and non-eruptive springs. During these early days, it would erupt at one-minute intervals. According to Marler, the 1959 Hebgen Lake earthquake affected Sponge, with its water level dropped eight feet. (YNPMC, YELL #114086.)

Pump Geyser is near Giantess and Sponge Geysers. The geyser erupts out of an 18-inch hole and makes a thumping sound. In 1990, Pump became a true geyser, with intervals and durations of a few seconds. The name Pump Geyser appears on a map in a 1912 *Haynes Guide*, so F. Jay Haynes may have named it. (YNPDSF, 10101, Frank Walker, 1978.)

Solitary Geyser is on the wooded hill well above Geyser Hill. In 1915, when Henry Brothers was permitted to utilize the water of "Solitary Spring" for the Geyser Baths, the reduction in water level caused what was a spring to become a geyser. However, after the bath was closed in 1948, Solitary Geyser continued to erupt, even to this day. (AandD.)

Lion Geyser, on Geyser Hill, is part of the Lion Group (pictured). This 1930s photograph shows signs identifying the group—from left to right, Little Squirt, Lioness, Big Cub, and Lion Geysers. Lion has been the most consistently powerful of the group, erupting a column of water 50 to 60 feet high. Lion probably got its name because it sounds like a lion's roar when it rapidly expels steam. (AandD.)

Big Cub Geyser is a member of the Lion Group. In the late 1940s, Marler witnessed a number of eruptions of Big Cub and Lioness Geyser, with Big Cub Geyser starting first and Lioness following within a couple of minutes. Only two eruptions are known since 1952: one in 1987 and one in 1998. (YNPDSF, 04864, Watson.)

This *1909 Campbell Guide* photograph shows a visitor walk being led by "Joe." Joe was the head porter at the Old Faithful Inn. His "Walks with Joe" usually left after lunch at the inn, started at Old Faithful Geyser and went north to Riverside Geyser. Here, his tour walked between Lion and Big Cub's cones on Geyser Hill. (*Campbell Guide,* 1909.)

Lion Geyser, shown here, erupts regularly with an initial eruption of 50–70 feet high for up to five minutes. It often erupts in sequence, with later eruptions producing the "lion's roar." Marler states that the three large Lion Group features show a subterranean connection, with Big Cub and/or Lioness Geysers only erupting when Lion is dormant. (Photograph by the authors, 1993.)

This view from 1884 shows an odd wooden structure in the Firehole River with Castle Geyser steaming in the background, often a next destination for visitors after seeing Geyser Hill. Although the purpose of this wood crib is not known, it could have been used as a personal bathhouse. (BYALE, 1066853, C.E. Watkins, 1884.)

Leaving Geyser Hill, many visitors walked to Castle Geyser, shown here in 1918 with Crested Pool in the foreground. Castle's cone has been described as a castle in ruins. The geyser has one of the most picturesque and perhaps oldest cones in Yellowstone. The cone is 12 feet high and 40 feet in diameter at the base. (Tammen, 1918.)

Castle's large cone, shown in this 1870s view, was covered with large geyserite formations of many sizes and shapes. Sadly, the cone has been nearly stripped by early visitors wishing to bring a piece of Yellowstone back home with them. Today, Castle erupts in a predictable manner, having first a water and then a steam phase with eruptions over 50 feet. (USGS, jwh01187, William Henry Jackson.)

In the 1930s, researchers Allen and Day described the opening at the top of Castle's cone (seen in this real-photo postcard) as "three feet across, circular, and cup shaped. The geyser tube opening can be sounded for only a few feet, but this narrow end evidently rises straight upward, for the jet is comparatively small and practically vertical."

Here, visitors mill around Castle Geyser during its water-phase eruption. Later, water turned to roaring steam. Old Faithful Inn can be seen, where the visitors' horse-drawn carriages likely were stationed. A major eruption of Castle attracted early visitors to the park for its height, duration, sound, and, under the correct lighting conditions, rainbows or moonbows in the water droplets. (Haynes postcard no. 129, 1910.)

Penta Geyser, between Castle and Grand Geysers, erupts from five separate vents, reaching 15–25 feet in height from its main vent, as seen in this 1870s William Henry Jackson photograph. Penta's eruptions are affected by eruptions of nearby Sawmill and Churn Geysers. Sawmill was dormant following the 1959 Hebgen Lake earthquake, and Penta Geyser played continually from five orifices for some time. (USGS, jwh00653.)

Grand Geyser, as shown in this William Henry Jackson photograph from 1872, erupts about 200 yards from the Firehole River against a bare hillside. Grand Geyser eruptions were irregular in the 1890s, with intervals between eruptions lasting 12–24 hours. However, they were described as among the finest in the park, having 10 or 12 distinct eruptions in series lasting up to 40 minutes. (USGS, jwh00668, 1872.)

In the 1930s, researchers described Grand Geyser as having a trumpet-shaped opening in the sintered, encrusted ground, seen here emptied after an eruption. Grand erupts from a shallow surface pool some 50 feet across with a relatively flat, broken, and inconspicuous sinter border. This flat, unremarkable pool seems to be a very plain setting for such a large geyser. (USGS, jwh0019, William Henry Jackson, 1872.)

This photograph by William Henry Jackson shows Grand, Turban, and Vent Geysers after an 1872 eruption of Grand, with steam from Vent (left) and Turban (center) shown. Grand Geyser is the empty pool to the right of Turban. Vent can reach 50–70 feet in height, and Turban can reach 5–10 feet above its rim. (USGS, jwh00194, 1872.)

Economic Geyser erupted to 30 feet from a pool north of Grand Geyser. One 1897 guidebook states that it was named from the fact that water fell back into the crater and disappeared, so the geyser had no overflow and reused its water. In the 1890s, the geyser erupted about every six minutes and was called "Young Faithful" by some. (Haynes postcard no. 202, 1915.)

In the early days of the park, Economic Geyser was a visitor favorite because of its regularity and height. In 1901, visitors would often stay and watch Economic erupt before having lunch, as shown in this photograph. Today, Economic rarely erupts. (Matteson postcard no. 209.)

Daisy Geyser, north of Castle on the paved path, is described in a 1912 *Haynes Guide* as a reliable geyser with eruptions occurring every one-half to two hours. It remains regular today, erupting to 75 feet. Marler photographed this eruption in 1960. Dr. Peale in the 1878 USGGS saw Daisy erupt, but due to name confusion he called it "Comet." (YNPDSF, 05083, George Marler, 1960.)

Splendid Geyser, photographed here by Marler, is located west of Daisy Geyser and was seen in eruption as early as the 1870s. An early visitor to Yellowstone was Windham Thomas Wyndham-Quin, the Earl of Dunraven, who saw an eruption in 1874 and describes it in *The Great Divide*. Splendid is much less active than Daisy, but it can reach 200 feet or more in height. (YNPDSF, 05192, George Marler.)

Visitors observe Splendid Geyser's crater. According to an 1886 book by W.H. Dudley, an early visitor said that "we were getting discouraged, beginning to think that the old adage regarding a 'watched pot' might also apply to a geyser, when something about its appearance attracted my friend's attention. He commenced backing away, saying 'I believe this thing's going off.'" (YNPMC, YELL #148131, 1896.)

This 1918 view of Giant Geyser in full eruption shows visitors near the large cone. Giant Geyser, east of Splendid, is one of the tallest geysers in the world. According to an 1897 visitor guidebook, "The platform of deposit upon which the cone stands is about seventy-five feet in diameter. The cone is broken on the west side from the apex nearly to the base, affording a good view of the interior of the crater, which is almost constantly in a state of turbulent boiling and splashing. In 1881 the break in the cone was not nearly so large, not more than half its present proportion, the enlargement being without a doubt the result of an unusual violent eruption." In a 1912 *Haynes Guide*, it is described as playing to 250 feet in height for an hour and a half. The greatest height is reached early in the eruption. (Tammen, 1918.)

Visitors seen—probably in the early 1900s—in this real-photo postcard are gathered on Giant Geyser's cone, which must have been a common activity in the very early park days. During the Washburn Expedition's stay in the Upper Geyser Basin in 1870, members saw eruptions of most of the major geysers, including Giant. They gave this geyser its name because of the power of its eruption.

Giant Geyser's cone, seen here, is 10 feet high with one side broken off, exposing its channel, which is 4 feet across. Dr. Hayden in 1872 described the cone as "situated on a platform of geyserite, which rises four feet above the surrounding level and has a circumference of 342 yards." Today, boardwalks keep Giant Geyser's unique cone and park visitors safe. (USGS, jwh00736, William Henry Jackson, 1870s.)

Oblong Geyser, another visitor favorite, is near the Firehole River a short distance south from Giant Geyser. The oblong crater, as seen here in 1887, is 30 by 50 feet in size, giving the geyser its name. The crater is exposed after an eruption, showing globular masses. (Haynes, 1887.)

Grotto Geyser, located northwest of Giant Geyser, has one of the most curious geyser cones. The cone has strange, cave-like openings and pillars. In the 1880s, eruptions like this one took place about four times a day. Geyser observers think that Grotto and Giant are connected underground due to the effects the activity of each has on the other. (Haynes, 1887.)

Grotto Geyser was just off the main road until the road was rerouted in 1971–1972. It was, and still is, a visitor favorite, erupting for 30 minutes or more with immense volumes of steam escaping with great force. About 20 feet from Grotto, on the same sinter platform, is a smaller erupting geyser called Rocket Geyser. (Tammen, 1918.)

Members of the Washburn party named Grotto Geyser in 1870. From the earliest days, the intricate shape and pillars have fascinated visitors. Even when it was not erupting, early park visitors stopped to look at this odd creation of nature. Today, boardwalks and paths keep visitors off this feature, protecting the cone from further damage and the visitors from burns. (YNPMC, YELL #147820, c. 1875.)

Riverside Geyser was named by members of the USGGS after they observed it erupting out over the Firehole River. Early guidebooks describe Riverside as one of the most spectacular geysers in the park, and one that should be seen by every visitor. In the 1890s, a wooden bridge crossed the Firehole River close to Riverside, as seen here. (Detroit postcard no. 12044, 1910.)

Marler described Riverside Geyser in the 1950s: "When it comes to setting, Riverside is certainly one of the most fortunate among the geysers. Its position on the very edge of the Firehole River, with the column of water arching over the stream, plus the coniferous-forest background, make it a photographer's delight." Note the visitor standing on Riverside's cone. (YNPMC, YELL #148074, Haynes, 1890.)

As described in the 1897 *Haynes Guide*, "A short distance above the wagon bridge across the Firehole River is seen the Riverside Geyser, whose cone is close to the water's edge . . . An overflow of water from the lower crater is a certain indication of approaching activity beginning about 30 minutes prior to eruptions." (Tammen, 1918.)

The 1870 Washburn party named Fan and Mortar Geysers. In 1880, Reverend Stanley wrote, "This is one of the prettiest spouters in the region. Its machinery is surely the most complicated of any, and, having five distinct orifices, it sends up as many jets of water and steam, sometimes reaching an altitude of one hundred feet." (YNPDSF, 07487, J. Schmidt, 1977.)

Beyond Fan and Mortar Geysers is Morning Glory Pool, described as world famous from the earliest days. As seen in and described on this 1918 Tammen photograph, the pool was "funnel-shaped to depth and filled to the rim with transparent blue water, which under full sunshine was magnificent to behold." The Grand Loop Road, before its relocation, can be seen next to the pool in this view. (Tammen, 1918.)

The old road, now a footpath, continued north of Morning Glory and passed above Artemisia Geyser (pictured). Marler stated that Artemisia "has one of the largest craters of any thermal spring in Yellowstone . . . nearly circular . . . about 50 feet in diameter. The unusual sinter deposits which gird the crater on the south and southwest represent the nicest natural ornamentation in the park." (Haynes, 1887.)

Biscuit Basin, a part of the Upper Geyser Basin north of Artemisia Geyser, was named for the geyserite formations surrounding Sapphire Pool, as shown above. According to an 1897 guidebook, "The principal attraction of Biscuit Basin is Sapphire Pool . . . Hundreds of small, symmetrical, biscuit like knobs of olive-green formation surround the spring . . . The constant ebb and flow of its waters have produced this peculiar formation." Four weeks after the 1959 Hebgen Lake earthquake, Sapphire Pool began to have enormous eruptions, similar to the one shown at right. These eruptions reached 125 feet and destroyed the "biscuits." Ranger Lowell B. Biddulph, in a handwritten article titled "The Birth of Sapphire Geyser," describes it: "Great surging waves of hot water rushed down . . . carrying innumerable chunks of broken geyserite." (Above, Detroit chromolithograph no. 53333, 1902; right, courtesy of Avon Leeking, 1960.)

Black Sand Basin is located west of the main Upper Geyser Basin. Cliff Geyser (pictured, but incorrectly labeled on the postcard) is a regular performer in the basin. Another popular feature near Cliff Geyser is Emerald Pool, a hot spring with a deep green color in the center. Sunset Lake is also at Black Sand Basin and has an irregular history of eruptions. (Tammen postcard no. 8524, 1908.)

Seen here, Sunset Lake erupts to 20 feet behind an also erupting Cliff Geyser. In 1870, Lt. Gustavus C. Doane described Sunset as "a lake of Bluestone water, a hundred feet in diameter." Marler reported that Sunset had a major eruption after the 1959 Hebgen Lake earthquake. Algae in the runoff channel was killed, and wave action washed away pieces of sinter. (Courtesy of Udo Freund.)

Rainbow Pool, seen here, is a few feet south of Sunset Lake. When it was named and by whom are lost to history. Rainbow Pool erupted infrequently before the 1930s. Marler documents that "Rainbow Pool had a series of eruptions in 1940-41 and 1946-47. An eruption in 1973 may have been over 100 feet high." (Photograph by the authors, 2000.)

According to Marler, "with Old Faithful Geyser and Morning Glory Pool, [Handkerchief Pool] had shared the honor of being one of the three most popular of Yellowstone's highly publicized hydrothermal features." Until 1929, items such as handkerchiefs were placed in the pool, convective water currents drew them down below the surface, and they reappeared, coated with silica. (Tammen postcard no. 4500, 1922.)

At over nine feet tall, Lone Star Geyser, located three miles upstream on the Firehole River from Old Faithful, has one of the largest cones in the park. According to Marler, "It has one of the most distinctive and symmetrical cones of any geyser in the park." It is on a trail beginning at Kepler Cascades. (USGS, jwh00662, William Henry Jackson, 1870s.)

The Perozic brothers, visitors to the park, pose beside their Dodge truck while Lone Star Geyser erupts. The cone, once on the main road but now on a hiking and biking trail, varies from five to seven feet in diameter. At the top of the geyser are many small orifices and perforations; eruptions reach up to 45 feet high. (Courtesy of the Yellowstone Gateway Museum of Park County, Montana.)

Seven

West Thumb Geyser Basin

Early visitors arrived at West Thumb via stagecoach from the Old Faithful area. West Thumb is a four-by-five-mile bay in the western section of Yellowstone Lake. This area of the lake formed as an explosion crater within the larger Yellowstone caldera. The Washburn Expedition named West Thumb in 1870 based on its thumb-like projection of Yellowstone Lake. On its western shore lies a flat terrace sloping to the shoreline known as West Thumb Geyser Basin. West Thumb Geyser Basin is comprised of the Lower Group, Lake Shore Group, and Potts Hot Spring Basin and is the largest geyser basin on Yellowstone Lake. The sinter sheets that cover the ground in the basin extend into the lake. The area is covered by hot springs, a few geysers, paint pots, and some large deep pools. Fur trappers Warren Ferris and Osborne Russell visited this area in the 1830s. The Washburn party visited in 1870, and the features are described in detail in the 1878 *USGGS*. These springs were popular as a stopping place for early travelers. The 1878 *USGGS* states, "The locality is known as Hot Springs Camp and has become a favorite resting place for those who go to Yellowstone Lake from the Upper Geyser Basin."

This was the final geyser basin on the early tours around the Grand Loop Road. Visitors left West Thumb Geyser Basin to see Yellowstone Lake and to stay at Lake Hotel. After leaving the Lake Hotel, they traveled north, stopping briefly to see Mud Volcano, and then headed for the canyon area to see the Upper and Lower Falls of the Yellowstone River. After staying at the Canyon Hotel, the tours returned the visitors to their entrance station on their way home.

As roads improved, a military detachment was stationed at West Thumb from 1897 until 1904 to protect the park and to watch over visitors traveling the Grand Loop Road. Originally, these hardy soldiers stayed in tents, but in 1904, the West Thumb soldier station was erected, as shown in this photograph. (YNPDSF, 10644, Haynes, 1904.)

MUD SPRINGS.

Dr. Peale describes the Thumb Paintpots: "The mud puffs are situated in the bank of clay (to which their peculiar character is due) of bright pink and red colors. The basin is about 50 feet in diameter, and the center is a seething mass of very finely divided mud, which on drying is lighter in color, and becomes a hard mass resembling chalk." (1878 *USGGS*.)

The Thumb Paintpots change with time, weather conditions, and the amount of rain that has recently fallen, but they are always fun to see. As shown in this 1920s photograph, early travelers often wore suits when they visited Yellowstone. (AandD.)

The Thumb Paintpots have been a favorite with visitors for over 100 years. They resemble the Fountain Paint Pot. Allen and Day studied the area in the 1920s and determined that the area's pink and white tints are due to a shortage of sulphur. A liberal mix of sulphur would have changed the iron into pyrite and turned the mud gray. (Courtesy of Graham Meech, 2008.)

Perforated Pool, within the main or Lower Basin, is shown well below overflow and boiling. Pool water can rise and overflow into Yellowstone Lake, as well as have rare small eruptions to perhaps two feet in height. The pool was named in the 1950s for the holes on the bottom that allow gases to escape. (Photograph by the authors, 2010.)

Twin Geysers has a vague history, with reports of eruptions since the early 1900s. No one seems to know who named it or when. Recently, it has erupted irregularly, reaching heights of 70 to over 100 feet. In the 1930s, this geyser was called "Maggie and Jiggs" after characters in the comic strip *Bringing Up Father.* (YNPDSF, 05382, Lawrence Boe, 1975.)

Twin Geysers has two vents and can be the most spectacular geyser at West Thumb Geyser Basin. For many decades before the 1930s, this geyser erupted to less than four feet. Large eruptions began in the 1930s. In the late 1940s, eruptions of over 100 feet in height were seen. This photograph shows an eruption in 1999. (Courtesy of Ralph Taylor, 1999.)

Abyss Pool has been an active geyser since Yellowstone's early history. In 1871, Dr. Hayden visited this spring and thought it to be a most spectacular site. Known eruptions have occurred since the early 1900s, with some reaching 100 feet. Its most recent eruption was in 1992. This photograph shows the clear, deep, hot pool. (Photograph by the authors, 2010.)

Arthur L. Day photographed West Thumb and stated, "but the one most deserving attention, though without a name [now King Geyser], is a geyser of the fountain type in the northwest corner of the principal area. While the water rises only five or six feet, the tumultuous commotion of the hot splashing masses in its ample crater and its copious discharge are quite impressive." (AandD.)

Black Pool has been at times cool enough for cyanobacteria mats to grow on the edges of the pool, giving the water a dark orange/brown color. According to Lee Whittlesey, chief park naturalist Clyde M. Bauer named Black Pool for its dark color in 1937. Today, after a heating cycle, the pool is free of growth and is a brilliant blue. (Photograph by the authors, 2010.)

Fishing Cone, according to a 1917 *Haynes Guide*, was named by members of the 1871 USGGS and was famous for years. No visit to the park was complete unless this feature was seen. By 1917, the practice of cooking a fish in the cone was prohibited. (Tammen, 1918.)

In 1901, Olin Wheeler wrote, "Now he casts his hook into the lake. Only for a short time, though, for the trout swarm here and one is always ready to be fooled . . . Fresh from the lake, dangling on the hook, he is quickly dropped into the pool within the cone whereon the fisherman stands and presto in a twinkling he is boiled and ready to eat." (Tammen, 1918.)

A woman cooking her fish still on the line was a scene likely repeated many times in the early days. In this undated photograph, Fishing Cone is well above the level of Yellowstone Lake, but at times can be well below the lake level. Access to Fishing Cone is no longer permitted. (YNPMC, YELL #118592-2.)

High lake levels submerge Fishing Cone in Yellowstone Lake, as seen here. According to the USGS, the shoreline of Yellowstone Lake has been gradually changing. During the spring melt, water levels of the lake now often inundate the spring. In the 1920s and 1930s, the cone was known to erupt, but modern high lake levels have cooled the spring. (Photograph by the authors, 2005.)

Lakeshore Geyser, seen in eruption in 1909, is on the shore of Yellowstone Lake. In the spring, the vent can be covered by water and cannot then erupt. Usually, the cone is uncovered later in the summer or early fall. The geyser, erupting to 20–30 feet, was seen in eruption by the Hague Survey in 1889, according to Lee Whittlesey in an unpublished manuscript. (USGS, lec01099, E.C. LaRue.)

Reports of Lakeshore Geyser eruptions began in the late 1800s, but the geyser can only erupt when not submerged by the lake. This photograph was taken on August 8, 1911, with the name Lakeside Geyser written on the image. The US Bureau of Fisheries constructed the building in the background in 1904 for studies of the lake. (Courtesy of David Monteith.)

Allen and Day indicate that Lakeshore Geyser, located on Yellowstone Lake, "played rather frequently (about once an hour in 1932) from a symmetrical cone . . . to a height of 20 to 25 feet." The visitor is provided a unique view across the lake to the distant mountains. (YNPDSF, 11084, R. Robinson.)

Lakeshore Geyser is very similar to Fishing Cone and located close to it, about 16 feet from the shoreline of Yellowstone Lake. The crater is a circular hole four feet in diameter. When the cone is uncovered, the geyser is known to erupt from a few feet up to at least 30 feet in height, but is often submerged, as shown in the photograph. (Photograph by the authors, 2012.)

Big Cone, shown here in winter, is north of and near Fishing Cone. The cone is on a mound of sinter and is about 22 feet wide. The crater is circular with a diameter of two and a half feet and is located 22 feet offshore in Yellowstone Lake. (YNPDSF, 14691, Frank Bathis, 1979.)

Occasional Geyser is north of the main West Thumb Geyser Basin in the Lake Shore Group. Eruptions were first noted in the 1890s and continue today, with eruptions reaching 20 feet. Overflow from eruptions cascades into Yellowstone Lake. This geyser can be observed from a boat on the lake or from the overlook on the road. (YNPDSF, 05379, Herkenham.)

According to Lee Whittlesey's unpublished manuscript *Wonderland Nomenclature*, in 1886, geologist Walter Weed of the Hague survey first studied Occasional Geyser. Occasional is a cone-type geyser that rests on a thick layer of geyserite. Eruptions come from three orifices, and heights of up to 60 feet have been reported. (Photograph by the authors, 2006.)

T. Scott Bryan in *The Geysers of Yellowstone* describes Occasional Geyser: "It plays from a complex of vents, one of which is an extraordinarily smooth and perfectly round crater lined with tan, beaded geyserite . . . Eruptions generally recur every 20 to 35 minutes, . . . [lasting] 30 seconds to two minutes." (YNPDSF, 05378, D.J. Brown.)

North of Occasional Geyser is Lone Pine Geyser on Yellowstone Lake, north of the main West Thumb Geyser Basin. According to T. Scott Bryan in *The Geysers of Yellowstone*, eruptions of 70 to 80 feet in height have been reported. The first eruptions occurred in the 1970s, when it was named because of a nearby pine tree. (YNPDSF, 11082, John Tyers, 1974.)

Overhanging Geyser is also in the Lake Shore Group. It is strangely positioned on a large overhang about 10 feet above Yellowstone Lake. According to Lee Whittlesey in an unpublished manuscript, it has been known to erupt since the 1870s. The geyser is located about 400 yards north of Occasional Geyser. When the geyser erupts, its overflow cascades off the overhang into the lake. (Courtesy of T. Scott Bryan, 1980s.)

The *Anna* was the first boat on Yellowstone Lake and is shown here in an 1871 photograph by William Henry Jackson. The name was misspelled when manually added to the negative. The boat was named for Anna L. Dawes, daughter of a US senator, Henry L. Dawes of Massachusetts. James Stevenson and Henry Elliot are in the boat, according to Hiram Chittenden in *The Yellowstone National Park*. The boat was used for lake depth soundings. (YNPDSF, 17958.)

This 1901 view shows a camp, possibly a Wylie Camp, on the shore of Yellowstone Lake, with a dock and boat. The dock may have served the *Zillah*, a steamship built to transport visitors across Yellowstone Lake from West Thumb and Lake Hotel from 1891 to 1917. The *Zillah* was also used to tow a barge with buffalo to Dot Island in 1896. (Detroit personal mailing card, 1901.)

Early visitors arrived at West Thumb via stagecoach from the Old Faithful area. After seeing West Thumb Geyser Basin, visitors could continue on the stagecoach or board the steamship *Zillah*, or other boats launched by the concessionaires, to continue the journey across Yellowstone Lake to Lake Hotel. The boat dock was located near the south end of the geyser basin near Lakeside Spring. In the background of the photograph above and in the photograph below is the Thumb Lunch Station, designed by architect Robert Reamer and built in 1903. According to the *1915 Superintendent' Report*, "the excursion boat on Yellowstone Lake . . . is not part of the regular transportation of the park and an extra charge is made by the boat company for this service." (Above, courtesy of David Monteith; below, *Yellowstone Park*, NPRR, 1913.)

Two ladies approach the dock on the lake near West Thumb Geyser Basin, shown in this postcard from 1905. The steamship *Zillah* at the dock served visitors from 1891 until 1917. Other crafts sailed on Yellowstone Lake, and even fur trappers or American Indians may have floated "boats" on the lake, but the steamship *Zillah* was in use for many years. (Detroit private mailing card no. 8806.)

This 1912 photograph shows the *Zillah* docking and unloading visitors. The presence of a dock near Fishing Cone, from which the steamboat plied the waters of Yellowstone Lake, no doubt contributed to Fishing Cone's popularity. Visitors likely looked at the spring while waiting to board the boat tour to Dot Island and to Lake Hotel. (YNPMC, YELL #127728)

Stagecoach travelers and boat passengers leaving West Thumb Geyser Basin needed accommodations at the lake. Construction of Lake Hotel began in 1889, and the hotel opened in 1891, as shown above. The photograph below shows the Colonial look, a result of a face-lift that was completed in 1903–1904. According to the *1904 Superintendent's Report*, "it has all of the modern conveniences, including suites of rooms with baths attached. This is now the largest hotel in the park. It has 210 rooms and can accommodate 316 guests." After a stay at Lake Hotel, visitors loaded onto stagecoaches and traveled to the Canyon area for their final destination before returning to the railroad terminus where they began. (Above, *1901 Superintendent's Report;* below, Detroit postcard no. 8814, 1901.)

Between Lake and Canyon, tours stopped to see Mud Volcano, which is described in the first chapter. The final visitor stop was the Canyon Hotel, built to accommodate visitors wanting to see the spectacular Upper and Lower Falls of the Yellowstone. It began as a temporary prefabricated building in 1886, shown above, and was replaced in 1890 by the second Canyon Hotel, shown below. This hotel remained until 1911, when the third Canyon Hotel was built, incorporating the second hotel structure into the new Canyon Hotel. (Both, *A Miracle in Hotel Building,* J.H. Rafferty, 1912.)

The third Canyon Hotel was built over the winter of 1910–1911, as shown in the photograph above. Architect Reamer may be the man on the left in the photograph. With the second hotel incorporated into the new structure, the perimeter of the hotel became a mile around, as shown below. In *A Miracle in Hotel Building*, Rafferty quotes Robert C. Reamer, architect of the new Canyon Hotel as well as Old Faithful Inn, Mammoth Hot Springs Hotel, Lake Hotel, and many other buildings: "I built it in keeping with the place where it stands. Nobody could improve upon that. To be at discord with the landscape would be almost a crime. To try to improve upon it would be an impertinence." After visiting West Thumb Geyser Basin, the lake, and Upper and Lower Falls, travelers returned to Gardiner or another railroad terminus and left the park. (Above, YNPMC, YELL #134918; below, YNPDSF, 02769.)

Most early visitors arrived and departed Yellowstone via railroads. Between 1883 and 1937, rail service was built to provide access to five entrances: the northern entrance by 1883, seen above; the west by 1908, seen below; the east by 1912; the south by 1922; and the northwest by 1937, according to Thornton Waite in *Yellowstone by Train*. The last passenger service into Yellowstone through the town of West Yellowstone ended in 1960. After 1915, motorized travel brought visitors to all the major geyser basins. Many accommodations are available today. Xanterra Parks and Resorts operates nine lodges at Mammoth Hot Springs, Roosevelt, Canyon, Lake, Grant Village, and Old Faithful. Camping is available in five reservation-only campgrounds run by Xanterra, and in seven first-come, first-served campgrounds managed by the NPS. (Above, C.T. Company postcard no. A6863, 1910; below, Detroit postcard no. 70996, 1915.)

BIBLIOGRAPHY

Allen, E.T. and Arthur L. Day. *Hot Springs of the Yellowstone National Park*. Washington, DC: Carnegie Institution of Washington, 1935.

Bryan, T. Scott. *The Geysers of Yellowstone*. Boulder: University Press of Colorado, 2008.

Campbell, Reau. *Campbell's New Revised Complete Guide*. Yellowstone Park, WY: H.E. Klamer, 1909, 1914, and 1923.

Ferris, Warren Angus. *Life in the Rocky Mountains: a Diary of Wanderings on the sources of the Rivers Missouri, Columbia, and Colorado, 1830-1835*. Denver, CO: Fred A. Rosenstock, Old West Publishing Co., 1983.

Hayden, Ferdinand Vandiveer. *U.S. Geological and Geographical Survey of the Territories of Wyoming and Idaho*. Washington, DC: US Government Printing Office, 1871, 1872, and 1878.

Haynes, F. Jay. *The Yellowstone National Park in Photogravure*. Fargo, Dakota: F. Jay Haynes, 1887.

Marler, George D. *Inventory of Thermal Features of the Firehole River Geyser Basins and other Selected Areas of Yellowstone National Park*. Springfield, VA: NTIS, 1973.

Rafferty, J.H. *A Miracle in Hotel Building*. Yellowstone, WY: Yellowstone Park Company, 1912.

Riley, W.C. *Yellowstone National Park: The World's Wonderland*. Frankfurt, Germany: Charles Frey, 1889.

Stanley, Edwin J. *Rambles in Yellowstone*. New York: D. Appleton and Co., 1880.

Tammen, H.H. *The Wonders of Geyserland*. Denver, CO: H.H. Tammen, 1918.

Topping, E.S. *Chronicles of the Yellowstone*, 1883. Minneapolis: Ross & Haines, Inc., 1968.

Waite, Thornton. *Yellowstone by Train: A History of Rail Travel to America's First National Park*. Missoula, MT: Pictorial Histories Publishing Co., 2006.

Weed, Walter. *Geysers of the Yellowstone National Park*. Washington, DC: US Government Printing Office, 1929.

Wheeler, Olin. Wonderland Series: *6000 Miles Through Wonderland*, 1893; *Sketches of Wonderland*, 1895; *Wonderland 1896, 1902, 1903, 1904, 1905, 1906*. St. Paul, MN: Northern Pacific Railway.

White, Donald E., Hutchinson R.A., and T.E.C. Keith. *The Geology and Remarkable Thermal Activity of Norris Geyser Basin, Yellowstone National Park, Wyoming, USGS Professional Paper 1456*. Washington, DC: US Government Printing Office, 1988.

Whittlesey, Lee H. *Yellowstone Place Names*. Gardiner, MT: Wonderland Publishing, 2006.

———. *Wonderland Nomenclature*. Unpublished. Helena, MT: Montana Historical Society, 1988.